BLOODY

HISTORY

BUCKINGHAMSHIRE

A COOK'S BRITISH
HISTORY

OF

BUCKINGHAMSHIRE

BLOODY BRITISH HISTORY

HISTORY

BUCKINGHAMSHIRE

EDDIE BRAZIL

The
History
Press

First published in 2014

The History Press
The Mill, Brimscombe Port
Stroud, Gloucestershire, GL5 2QG
www.thehistorypress.co.uk

© Eddie Brazil, 2014

The right of Eddie Brazil to be identified as the Author
of this work has been asserted in accordance with the
Copyright, Designs and Patents Act 1988.

All rights reserved. No part of this book may be reprinted
or reproduced or utilised in any form or by any electronic,
mechanical or other means, now known or hereafter invented,
including photocopying and recording, or in any information
storage or retrieval system, without the permission in writing
from the Publishers.
British Library Cataloguing in Publication Data.
A catalogue record for this book is available from the British Library.

ISBN 978 0 7509 6023 6

Typesetting and origination by The History Press
Printed in Great Britain

CONTENTS

INTRODUCTION AND ACKNOWLEDGEMENTS

THE HISTORY OF Britain has generally been one of relative peace, innovation, triumph and victory interspersed with periods of calamity, catastrophe and bloody murder. One could say the history of Buckinghamshire has been no different. Yes, we can be proud that the county is the birthplace of the Paralympics, the Open University, the first Sunday schools and has such personalities and luminaries as John Milton, Jerome K. Jerome, Enid Blyton, Sir Lawrence Olivier, David 'Del Boy' Jason, and the exiled kings Zog of Albania and Louis XVIII of France as one-time residents.

Yet down the years Buckinghamshire has also seen its fair share of bloody battles, vicious murders, catastrophic disasters, devastating diseases, and enough oddballs and eccentrics to fill ten football pitches. If you, dear reader, are fascinated by the darker, more bizarre and downright peculiar aspects of the history of Buckinghamshire, then read on!

Perhaps it is no great credit to Buckinghamshire that a book of this kind could have been thrice the length. I have tried to include as broad a spectrum of the county's dark and weird side as possible, and I apologise if I have omitted any grisly deed or deadly act. Throughout the pages I have referred, where relevant, to locations and events outside of Bucks, as the history of the county is inextricably linked to the incidents, episodes and people who have shaped the history of Britain.

I hope you enjoy reading the book as much as I have had researching and writing it. I would like to thank Cate Ludlow, Naomi Reynolds and all at The History Press for their support; also my good friend Paul Adams for his help and encouragement. Finally, thanks to my wife, Sue, and my daughter, Rebecca, for their patience, sandwiches and beer.

Unless otherwise credited, all images are part of the author's or The History Press' collection.

43 BC–55 AD

BUCKINGHAMSHIRE V. THE ROMANS

THE COUNTY OF Buckinghamshire was created in the late ninth or early tenth century by the Anglo-Saxon king, Alfred the Great (reigned 871–899). The territory or shire, which took its name from the settlement (or 'ham') of Bucca's people, covers an area of 750 square miles and stretches some 52 miles from north to south and about 20 miles west to east. It is one of the smaller English shires and today its boundaries remain pretty much the same as those defined over 1,000 years ago.

Of course, in the beginning the area wasn't known as Buckinghamshire. Way back, before the Saxon Thane Bucca set up home on the banks of the River Great Ouse, and long before the quaint hamlets, picturesque villages and the rolling, leafy lanes made Bucks the most English of counties, this was an altogether different landscape – a harsh environment populated by an ancient people.

The last great Ice Age began to retreat from Britain after 10,000 BC. As the ice and tundra shrank northwards, a new terrain of woods, hills and river valleys was created. By 6,000 BC, the rising sea level finally severed Britain from mainland Europe and into this virgin landscape came hunter-gatherers of the Mesolithic (Middle Stone Age) period. Here they collected nuts and fruits, and hunted deer and wild boar. They were flint users, crafting axes, tools and spears, and evidence of their presence has been discovered all over the county, from Bow Brickhill in the north to Gerrards Cross and Chesham in the south.

These people were the early inhabitants of Buckinghamshire. Down the centuries they would be followed by many others, and all would leave evidence of their occupation upon the landscape and would help to shape the county we know today. Yet two peoples in particular would come to contest the ownership of what would become Buckinghamshire – and also the lordship of the whole of England. It would be a struggle to the death, and both sides were prepared to shed the blood of many to win.

By 100 BC, the Romans had forged an empire in the Mediterranean that stretched across most of Europe, North Africa and the Middle East up to the

The 5,000-year-old Neolithic Barrow on Whiteleaf Hill, near Princes Risborough.

Red Sea. The legions had conquered Gaul – modern-day France – and were poised, as many future armies would be, to cross the body of water which separates Britain from mainland Europe. However, one British tribe was determined to resist the seemingly unstoppable Roman war machine. These were the Catuvellauni, an ancient British people who, in 55 BC, controlled a vast area of southern Britain which included modern-day Buckinghamshire. If you had been resident in the Aylesbury Vale, the Chilterns or the beech woods of the southern half of the county 2,000 years ago, you could have counted yourself as one of the Catuvellauni.

They were a fierce, Celtic-speaking people, spiked – or long-haired – warrior race who painted their bodies in blue woad and charged into battle on foot or mounted on armoured war chariots. Their original capital was based at Wheathampstead in Hertfordshire, yet evidence of their presence in Buckinghamshire has been discovered at Fleet Marston near Aylesbury, High Wycombe and Gerrards Cross.

In 55 BC, under their king, Cassivellaunus, they expanded their territory by defeating their neighbouring tribes, the Trinovantes and the Attrebates. In battle, Cassivellaunus killed the pro-Roman Trinovante king, Imanuentius, forcing the slain monarch's son to flee to Gaul seeking the help of Roman general (and soon to be emperor) Julius Caesar. Caesar duly responded by crossing the Channel with 10,000 men, but his army was met by a coalition of tribes under the leadership of Cassivellaunus. According to Caesar, this coalition was defeated, and the Roman army returned to Italy shortly afterwards. However, this may not be an accurate portrayal of the situation, as Cassivellaunus remained in control of the southern half of the country after the Roman army had retreated.

A year later Caesar returned and this time defeated Cassivellaunus in a battle south of the Thames, probably near modern Brentford. The Catuvellauni and their allies were forced to fall back to their tribal capital, where they made a final stand but were defeated; Cassivellaunus subsequently sought peace. It was a victory for Caesar but appears to have been a hollow triumph for the Roman general, for soon after the battle he departed for Rome leaving the Catuvellauni the dominant tribe in the land.

Almost 100 years later the Romans again attempted to conquer Britain. In that time the Catuvellauni, under their king, Cunobelinus, the grandson

An idea of how the Celtic residents of early Buckinghamshire might have looked.

Earthen ramparts of the remains of the Catuvellauni capital at Wheathampstead in Hertfordshire.

of Cassivellaunus, had expanded their domain, spreading north towards Lincolnshire, south and east into modern-day Kent and Essex, and west to parts of what would become Gloucestershire. Their capital was moved, first to Verulamium (now St Albans), and then to Camulodunum (Colchester in Essex).

In AD 40 the son of Cunobelinus, Caratacus, became king and continued the strategy of subjugating the other British tribes. It was a military policy not lost on the Romans, who had been watching the progress of the battle-hardened Catuvellauni with increasing alarm from across the Channel in Gaul.

In AD 43 Emperor Claudius decided to check the aggression of the British tribe. He crossed the sea at the head of 40,000 troops. Much to the Romans' surprise, they landed unopposed on the south coast and proceeded to march inland, expecting every moment to be confronted by Caratacus – but the

The Emperor Claudius, who invaded Britain in AD 43.

Catuvellauni were nowhere to be seen; Claudius and his legions began to think that the conquest would be a walkover. However, Caratacus and his men were waiting for them. At the River Medway in Kent, the British tribe, their bodies painted in blue woad and driving their scythe-wielding chariots, engaged the Romans in a bloody two-day struggle. It was a vicious affair with no quarter given, yet gradually the legions began to gain the upper hand and force the Catuvellauni back. The brother of Caratacus, Togodumnus, was slain and slowly the tribesmen began to retreat. Caratacus organised line after line of defence, testing the Roman generals in a succession of battles which cost the legions considerable numbers of troops. Still the Romans advanced, and still Caratacus and his people fought on. Driven back to their territory in what would become Buckinghamshire, they

Memorial detailing the defeat of Cassivellaunus, King of the Catuvellauni by Julius Caesar in 54 BC.

Caractacus, King of the Catuvellauni, in captivity and brought before the Roman Emperor Claudius.

made a last stand, but without the support of those tribes which had gone over to the Romans the Catuvellauni were vanquished.

Caratacus managed to escape the victorious legions and swore continued defiance. Fleeing to the wilds of the mountains of Wales, he organised further resistance to the Roman invasion. Once again he gave battle, and once again he and his allies were defeated – yet still the British chieftain refused to submit to the Roman commander, Publius Ostorius Scapula. He fled to the territory of the northern tribe, the Brigantes, to seek the help of their queen, Cartimandua.

But it was the end for the defiant king of the Catuvellauni; Cartimandua had allied herself with the Romans and betrayed him. He was captured, clapped in chains, and he and his family were shipped off to Rome to be paraded through the city in humiliating defeat. Even in this desperate situation, the British chieftain remained defiant. Emperor Claudius granted him one last speech and such was the passion and power of the Catuvellaunian leader's words that the Romans were stunned into silence. Emperor Claudius was so impressed that he freed Caratacus and his family, and they remained in Rome as free citizens.

For the other British tribes there would be a different outcome. A new culture and age was dawning. Those tribes who had gone over to the Romans in the hope of retaining some form of independence and autonomy were quickly disillusioned.

The village of Gerrards Cross, near Denham, is often associated with leafy suburbia, stock-brokers and chartered accountants. Yet this straight-laced part of middle England, only 20 miles from central London, contains the largest Iron Age hill fort in Buckinghamshire. Its double row of ditches and ramparts covers an area of 22 acres and were constructed by the Catuvellauni people over 2,000 years ago. In the late seventeenth century the notorious 'hanging' Judge Jeffreys lived in a house on the south-east corner of the fort. The house was demolished in the nineteenth century.

The Iceni rebellion in AD 60 under Queen Boudicca was defeated and the Roman Empire began its 400-year rule of the province of Britannia.

The Roman historian Tacitus recorded that Caratacus was the most formidable fighter the legions had encountered in Britain. One wonders what might have been achieved if all of the British tribes had allied in battle under his command. He was a true warrior of ancient Buckinghamshire.

AD 450–1066

SAXON TERROR!

ROMAN POWER BEGAN to decline in Britain about AD 409. Continued raids upon the eternal city forced the legions to abandon the province of Britannia and return home to defend Rome, leaving the Romano-British at the mercy of increasing attacks by Saxon pirates from Demark and Germany, Picts from the north and Irish raiders from the west. The British king, Vortigen, sought the help of Anglo-Saxon mercenaries in quelling the bloody incursions and the legendary Hengist and Horsa helped stem the tide of the hordes streaming across the abandoned Hadrian's Wall. Yet it was soon to be the emerging English who would be fighting the Romano-British for control.

The Saxon mercenaries saw what riches the land of Britannia contained, and wanted it for themselves. They sent word back across the North Sea to their kinfolk, and soon a mass migration of Angles, Saxons and Jutes from Northern Germany and Denmark arrived on the eastern shores of the abandoned Roman province.

Most of them came for plunder and war, but others would settle peacefully in the new land. Many would marry into Romano-British families and adopt existing customs and names, and throughout Buckinghamshire one can still find place names that are of British rather than Anglo-Saxon origin.

However, back in the fifth century the struggle for control of Britain between Saxons and the Romano-British continued in a series of bloody battles. Out of this misty period of history known as the Dark Ages emerged a legendary warrior by the name of Arturious. As the Saxons moved further west into Britain they were met in battle in about AD 500 by King Arthur at Badon Hill, probably in modern-day Wiltshire. Here the invaders were halted, but only for a time.

The invaders not only came with fire and sword but also with a new religion. Roman Britain was a Christian province, but the Anglo-Saxons worshiped gods including Woden, Thunor and Twi (from where derive our modern names for Wednesday, Thursday and Tuesday). Monasteries across the island were attacked, including one battle in Cheshire where the Saxons massacred 1,200 monks. They also practiced blood sacrifice, and many Saxon graves have been discovered throughout Buckinghamshire with the remains of mutilated or decapitated skeletons. In numerous burials the headless bodies of women were laid on top of the male corpses, suggesting that the spouse of a dead warrior was also ritualistically killed to accompany her husband to the next world. Other burial sites have revealed that some females – possibly slaves – were buried alive. It seems that if the Angles and Saxons were not slaughtering monks then they were putting the native inhabitants to the sword.

During the reign of West Saxon King Cerdic (AD 519–534) the Romano-British were defeated at the battle of Chearsley, near Long Crendon. In AD 571 the English captured Aylesbury, one of the last remaining British strongholds, when it was stormed by Cutwulph, brother of Ceawlin, king of the West Saxons.

Despite this unremitting violence, in the year 597 Pope Gregory, in an attempt to guide the bloodthirsty pagans towards a more peaceful existence, sent St Augustine to convert the heathen English to Christianity. In the early seventh century Aethelberht of Kent was the first Anglo-Saxon king to be baptised and accept Christianity. Although most of the pagan kings would eventually follow, some held on to their pagan beliefs, in particular the kingdom of Mercia.

Between AD 500 and 850, what would become England was divided into seven separate kingdoms, known as the Heptarchy. It consisted of East Anglia, Mercia, Northumbria, Kent, Wessex, Essex and Sussex. Over the years each would experience supremacy and subjugation. However, by the

year AD 796, the kingdom of Mercia, or Middle Angles, which stretched from the River Humber in the north to the Tamar in the south west, became the dominant force in England. The county of Buckinghamshire would eventually emerge from the territory of Mercia more by necessity than design.

After AD 800, following years of petty squabbling, the kingdoms of England were forced to unite to face a common enemy. In that year terrible portents appeared over Northumbria

Alfred the Great, King of the Anglo-Saxons, who saved England from total Danish conquest.

when heathens destroyed God's church in Lindisfarne by rapine and slaughter. The Vikings had arrived!

Throughout the ninth century, England was continuously raided by the Danes, and one by one the English kingdoms fell under the yoke of Viking power. The year AD 870 was the low-water mark in the history of Anglo-Saxon England. With all the other kingdoms having fallen, Wessex alone – under its king, Alfred the Great – still resisted. In May 878 the king emerged from retreat in the Somerset marshes and gathered an army which would be England's last chance to prevent complete Danish conquest. At the Battle of Edington the Danes were defeated and pursued back to their stronghold at Chipperham. Here they were starved into submission and surrendered. One of the conditions of their defeat was that they should become Christians and soon after, the Danish king, Guthrum, and twenty-nine of his chief men, were baptised at Alfred's court, with Alfred receiving Guthrum as his spiritual son.

Yet this peace lasted only until 884, when Guthrum once again attacked Wessex. Alfred defeated him, but had to accept that the Danes were in England to stay. A treaty outlined the boundaries of the territory, which came to be known as the Danelaw, and allowed for Danish

Coin of Edward the Elder, Alfred's son.

If the Anglo-Saxons were panicked by the sight of a Viking ship appearing over the horizon, just imagine how they felt about the famous warriors known as berserkers. These crazy Norsemen attacked in an uncontrollable, trance-like fury built up in the hours before a battle. It is believed that they ate drug-laced foods to further induce a state of intoxication. Their one goal was to earn a glorious death so they could enter the Viking heaven, Valhalla. The phrase 'to go berserk' is derived from their behaviour.

Although the majority of Buckinghamshire place names are Anglo-Saxon in origin, there remain a scattering of Brythonic (or British) place names throughout the county, which suggest that an enclave of Romano-British people still dwelt in the Chilterns long after their kinfolk had fled west to Cornwall, Wales or across the sea to Brittany. The villages of Penn, Wendover, Chalfont and Kimble are all Celtic in origin, as are the Rivers Thames, Thame and Ouse. The Anglo-Saxon word for 'stranger' or 'foreigner' was *wilisc* and it is from this that present-day Wales derives its name, although the Welsh would no doubt prefer their Celtic title, *cymru*, meaning fellow countrymen.

self-rule in the region. The region was roughly the area to the north of a line drawn between London and Chester. Gradually Alfred began to take back those parts of Eastern England occupied by the Danish. In 886 he captured London, and after AD 900 established the Shire, or territory of Buckingham, as a bulwark against further Viking attacks.

In the year 900 Alfred's son, Edward the Elder, became king, and succeeded in pushing back the boundaries of the Danelaw and forcing the Danes to accept him as their overlord. In 914 King Edward and a Saxon army encamped at Buckingham, which had been made a buhr (or fortified stronghold), for four weeks to oppose continued threats from the Vikings.

Edward's heir, Athelstan, who reigned from 925–939, extended the boundaries of England to their furthest extent yet. In 927 he retook York from the Danes and forced the submission of the Scottish and Welsh kings. In 937 he consolidated his power by defeating a combined army of Danes, Scots and Irish at the Battle of Brunanburh in the north of the country, and was recognised as the first king of all the English.

Despite future setbacks from further Danish attacks, and invasion in 1066 by the Normans, the nation of England, its language, people and culture had been firmly established, and would withstand, absorb and supersede its new French-speaking aristocratic rulers.

AD 1348–1666

THE BLACK DEATH

THERE WAS NO more deadly or devastating disease known to medieval Britain than bubonic plague. Normally fatal, it was no discriminator of class, age, health or wealth. There was no cure, and once infected the victim often had but days to live – in some instances, only hours. Once contracted, black 'buboes'

A dramatic woodcut depicting death taking a young victim. (With kind permission of the Thomas Fisher Rare Book Library, University of Toronto)

(blackish, gangrenous pustules, some as big as apples) would begin to appear under the armpits and around the groin. Dark blotches appeared on the arms, thighs or other parts of the body, caused by haemorrhages under the skin. With the swellings came fever and an agonising thirst. In some cases the sufferer would spit blood, and their sweat, excrement and breath gave off an overpowering stench.

The genesis of the disease is almost as abhorrent as the symptoms. Plague is carried by bacteria which normally live in the digestive tract of fleas – most especially the fleas of the black rat, a creature which often lives close to humans. The bacterium multiplies in the flea's stomach, eventually causing a blockage, and so while feeding, the flea regurgitates huge quantities of the bacteria – straight into its host. This terrifying disease is said to have entered Britain in October 1348 at Weymouth in Dorset, and with ruthless rapidity made its way across England.

In 1349 the plague struck in Buckinghamshire, causing heavy mortality in the Buckingham area, especially among the clergy and members of monastic orders. Virtually all of the community at Luffield Priory, on the Buckinghamshire/Northants border, perished. By the early sixteenth century there were probably fewer people living in the north of the county than in Roman times, as those who cared for the sick and dying were themselves struck down. Deserted and depopulated villages throughout Buckinghamshire – such as Dadford, Boycott, Haveringdon and Bredingcote – may give clues to the destructive nature of the pestilence. In the two years in which the plague ran riot an estimated 3 million people died in England. London alone lost 70,000 of its population. By 1350 the epidemic had dissipated, but it returned to cause more death and misery in 1361, and again in 1369. Between 1430 and 1480 it carried off as much as 20 per cent of the populace.

During the seventeenth century, plague returned once more to Buckinghamshire. In 1603 it hit the village of Wing, near Aylesbury, with particular venom. In 1617 at High Wycombe 112 people were struck down with the disease. It was to cause more terror in 1665 when it once again broke out in Wycombe; 96 residents perished, and a further 101 the following year. Fenny Stratford recorded 109 deaths in 1665, whilst Bletchley had six times the usual numbers of fatalities.

Some Buckinghamshire towns, such as Amersham, seem to have escaped the worst of the plague; this may be due to the building of a 'pest house' just outside the town on Gore Hill in 1625.

A dramatic view of the 'death carts' which were so terrible a part of this epidemic.

Potentially infected strangers coming to Amersham in times of pestilence were isolated there, together with any unfortunate townspeople who were thought to have contracted the disease.

In the absence of a method of defeating the disease, patients were subjected to barbaric means of treatment that included inducing vomiting and bloodletting. Some of the sick would be wrapped in a blanket and drenched in cold water. Perhaps the most bizarre remedy was to cut open a live pigeon from breast to back; the bird was broken open and, whilst the poor creature was still alive, its flesh was applied to the swellings on the skin of the patient. Given such treatments, death's arrival may have seemed like a sweet release. Unfortunately, the victim's dignity was not usually restored at death, as the corpses were unceremoniously thrown into hastily dug pits and covered with quicklime.

A 'Dance of Death' woodcut showing an abbot being carried off by death. (With kind permission of the Thomas Fisher Rare Book Library, University of Toronto)

AD 1455–1485

THE WARS
OF THE ROSES

IN 1483, IN AN UNASSUMING house in the High Street of an ordinary Buckinghamshire town, an uncle took charge of his young nephew and escorted him off to reside in a new home. The uncle was Richard III, and the boy was headed for the Tower of London. He would never be seen alive again.

The Wars of the Roses could be seen as a kind of medieval Mafia war: two opposing families fighting for control of England. Mob-style hits on those persons who were viewed as obstacles were common. As they say, it was business.

The origins of the conflict are convoluted, to say the least, but in essence it was a struggle for the throne of England fought between supporters of two rival branches of the royal House of Plantagenet, the Houses of Lancaster and York. The wars ground on, with many bloody battles, until Edward IV died in 1483. Edward had two sons, 12-year-old Edward and 9-year-old Richard. After his father's death, preparations began for the young Edward's coronation and so he travelled with Earl Rivers and Sir Richard Grey – uncles on his mother's side – from Ludlow Castle

towards London, stopping at Stony Stratford. It was here, in the Rose and Crown inn (which still stands in the High Street), that the royal entourage was met by the forces of Richard, Duke of Gloucester, later Richard III. He was the little boy's uncle on their father's side.

Rivers and Grey were arrested and quickly executed, and Prince Edward was taken into Richard's custody. After spending the night in the inn, Edward

King Richard III.

The Rose and Crown Inn, now a private house, at Stony Stratford, where Richard III took custody of his nephew in 1483.

was escorted to London and lodged in the Tower, where his younger brother was soon to join him. Preparations then began for Edward's coronation, but it was never to occur. Instead, the coronation of Richard III followed in June 1483, and the two young princes were quietly forgotten. Their fate has never been discovered, but the most likely explanation for their disappearance is that they were murdered. One contemporary Portuguese codex claims that the boys were handed over to Henry Stafford, 2nd Duke of Buckingham, who had them starved to death – though many other theories exist. Stafford himself later rebelled against Richard III, and he in his turn was captured and beheaded, as were many other nobles who opposed the crowning of the new king (including

William Lord Hastings, who was lured to a council meeting and then executed on Tower Green).

Richard was now free to rule, but support began to gather around the Duke of Richmond, Henry Tudor, the senior Lancastrian claimant to the throne. In August 1485 he landed in force at Milford Haven in Wales and made his way across England to Leicester, gathering men as he went. King Richard met him in the Battle of Bosworth, where he was killed; Shakespeare has him crying, 'A horse, a horse, my kingdom for a horse.' Tradition has it that his crown was found in a hawthorn bush on the battlefield and placed upon Henry Tudor's head with the proclamation, 'The king is dead. Long live King Henry!'

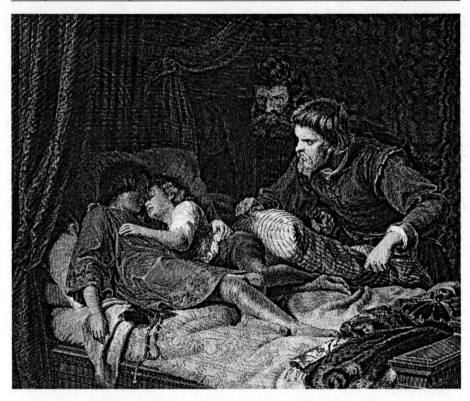

One version of the death of the Princes in the Tower, showing them about to be smothered.
Many believe this was on the orders of their uncle, Richard III.

The body of Richard III was stripped naked, placed over a horse and taken to Leicester, where it was unceremoniously thrown into the River Soar. However, in 2012 the remains of the king were discovered by archaeologists beneath a car park, formerly the site of a medieval priory, in the centre of the city.

AD 1521

BURNED AT THE STAKE

IT IS A commonly held belief that those found guilty of witchcraft in sixteenth- and seventeenth-century England suffered death by being burned at the stake. Although many women were accused of being in league with the horned one between 1440 and 1650 – and were either hanged, drowned, strangled or had their tongues pulled out – only three women convicted of witchcraft were burnt, and all three were strangled to death before being set ablaze.

Ironically, those in England who went to the stake were not disciples of Satan but devout followers of Christ. And they were set alight by other equally staunch Christians. It was all over the trifling matter of who could own and read the Bible.

The Protestant Reformation had caused a religious schism throughout a mainly Catholic Europe. What had started as a protest at the corruption of the Catholic Church soon began to embrace wider issues, one of which was the translation of the Bible into English. This was strongly rejected by the estab-lished Church of the day: priests, bishops and cardinals were viewed as the true intermediaries between man and God, and the sole exponents of his word.

In the early sixteenth century Amersham, in the south of Buckinghamshire, was a hotbed of Lollardism. The name Lollard was a contemptuous term for a follower of John Wycliffe, a fourteenth-century theologian, reformer, translator of the Bible into English and vigorous attacker of the abuses of the Church of Rome. When Henry IV usurped the throne in 1399, he passed a Statute that gave authority to bishops to punish those who were dissenters. If people were found guilty of heresy, which included owning

Not a lot of people were burnt at the stake in medieval England, for a very good reason; it was too expensive. Hanging was much more economical, as one rope could despatch any number of persons. When Isabel Cockie was burnt to death in 1596 her funeral pyre cost 100 shillings and 4 pennies, the equivalent of more than £1,000 in today's money.

and reading a Bible in English, they were condemned to be burned at the stake. Although Wycliffe himself died peacefully in 1384, many of his followers were much less lucky; Amersham saw a dozen or more people connected with the Lollard movement executed between 1414 and 1532. In 1414 four men from Amersham and one from Great Missenden were executed for adhering to Wycliffe's heretical views.

The Lollards referred to themselves as the 'just fast men' or 'known men', because of their steadfast allegiance to God. However, following the executions at Amersham, the unrest quietened and many of Wycliffe's supporters were forced into hiding. In around 1500 there

St Mary's church, Amersham, where the Lollards were tried and found guilty of heresy.

LOLLARD TORTURES

As well as executions, many Buckinghamshire believers were burned on the cheek or imprisoned. One 'Father Rogers' was in the bishop's prison for fourteen weeks, where he was 'so cruelly handled with cold, hunger and irons' that after his release he was 'so lame in his back, that he could never go upright as long as he lived'.

Fifteenth-century Castle House in Buckingham is said to be haunted by the ghost of a priest. His apparition has been seen gliding along a corridor which leads to a priest's hole, a place which proved to be his grave. In 1908 the house was being renovated when a small chamber was found hidden beneath the floor of the upper storeys directly over the Great Parlour. Within were found the bones of a man, along with a crucifix, rosary and some other belongings. It was from the time of the discovery of the corpse that the haunting began.

The clergyman is thought to have been Father Thomas, who administered Mass and confession to Catherine of Aragon (who had come to Buckingham in the latter part of the 1520s while her husband, King Henry VIII, was seeking grounds for divorce). One day Thomas simply vanished; his bones remained hidden for nearly 400 years. The great fire of 1725, which swept through Buckingham, destroyed nearly every building in the town except Castle House.

Catherine of Aragon, who came to Buckinghamshire seeking sanctuary. Whilst she was here her confessor was murdered.

was a Lollard revival in the Chilterns, and while most sympathisers recanted their beliefs when under pressure, others refused and went to stake. Among those charged and found guilty was William Tylsworth of Amersham. He refused to recant, and in 1506 was sentenced to be burned to death. The savagery of the time and the hatred towards dissenters is reflected in the fact that Tylsworth's own daughter, Joan, was made to light the fire that killed him. Other Amersham Lollards who suffered martyrdom for their beliefs were Robert Cosin, burned at Buckingham in 1506; Thomas Chase, strangled and beaten to death in a wood near Wooburn in 1514; and Thomas Mann, burned at the stake in London in 1518.

In 1521 John Longland was appointed Bishop of Lincoln and Confessor to King Henry VIII. To gain favour with his new royal master, a fresh round of heresy trials was embarked upon.

In that same year, six men and one woman from Amersham were put on trial in St Mary's church for Lollardy. None recanted their belief that they had the right to read and interpret the Holy Scripture and to worship God according to their conscience. They were found

Martyrs' Memorial commemorating the execution of nine Lollards on a hill outside Amersham.

guilty and taken from the church to a hill high above the town where each was burned at the stake. The most savage and heartbreaking of the executions was that of John Scrivener: his young children were forced to light their father's fire.

Thomas Harding, the last of the Lollard Martyrs, was burned at Chesham in 1532. As the flames licked higher, and the poor man writhed in pain, one of the horrified spectators took pity on the wretched soul and threw a log at him that 'dashed out his brains', sparing him the prolonged agony of his fiery end.

In 1931 a memorial in the shape of a giant, granite obelisk was erected on a hill overlooking Amersham to commemorate those who had suffered for their religious beliefs. It stands just 100 yards from where their execution pyres were lit, and looks over a town and countryside mostly unchanged since the sixteenth century. It was the final view for a dying man back in a savage and intolerant time.

AD 1605

REMEMBER, REMEMBER THE FIFTH OF NOVEMBER

Sir Everard Digby of Gayhurst. He paid with his life for treason.

THERE WERE THIRTEEN of them. An inauspicious number, if you were of a superstitious persuasion. Yet this baker's dozen of Catholic conspirators were determined men, firm in their faith, and ready to strike a blow for their beliefs. Their plot was planned in meticulous detail. All they had to do was rent a cellar under the House of Commons, fill it with thirty-six barrels of gunpowder, wait for the king and his court – together with the assembled Members of Parliament – to take their seats, light the fuse, and watch as London's night sky lit up with the roar and flash of an almighty explosion. With the king dead, they would stage an uprising in the country, put the dead monarch's daughter on the throne and return Britain to the Catholic fold. What could go wrong?

As we know, everything went wrong. The plot was betrayed, and the person responsible for detonating the explosives was discovered, arrested and tortured. From his limp body was extracted a confession which brought the plan crashing down on his fellow conspirators – who would ultimately pay the price for their treason.

Guy Fawkes is probably the only Gunpowder Plot conspirator most of us can name. Yet he was only a minor member of the conspiracy to assassinate King James I (VI of Scotland). The brain behind the plot was Robert Catesby, a well-to-do gentleman of Warwickshire. In 1593 he became connected, through marriage, to the Tyringham family of north Buckinghamshire, and across the valley from Tyringham was Gayhurst Manor, the home of Sir Everard Digby. Like Catesby, he had married into money, having wed Mary Mulsho, daughter of William Mulsho, lord of the manor of Gayhurst. Catesby and Digby soon became friends. They were both young, ambitious, and most importantly, Catholic.

When James I became king in 1603, Britain was a Protestant country that had seen decades of tension and violence between Catholics and the Protestants.

It was hoped the Scottish king would take a more tolerant attitude to Catholicism, but it was not to be and the faith was still suppressed. James increased penalties on those who still practised the religion, and discontent grew – to the extent that some Catholics were willing to take extreme measures. Two of those men were Robert Catesby and Everard Digby. Even though Digby had been knighted by King James, he disagreed passionately with the monarch's policies towards his faith.

The plot to remove King James from the throne was mostly concocted in the gatehouse of Catesby's home at Ashby St Ledger in Northamptonshire. But on several occasions the two men were joined by their fellow conspirators, including Guy Fawkes, at Gayhurst. Digby contributed £1,500 to the plan and, after the king and his court

Portrait of the Gunpowder conspirators. From left to right: Bates, Robert Winter, Christopher Wright, John Wright, Thomas Percy, Guy Fawkes, Robert Catesby and Thomas Winter.

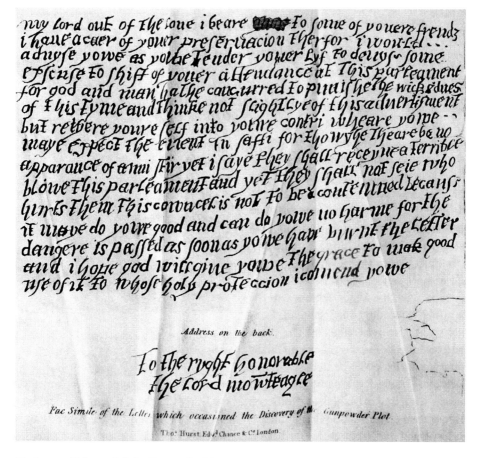

The letter which revealed the Gunpowder Plot.

had been blown sky high, he was to head for the West Country and raise a Catholic uprising.

The plot to restore Catholicism to Britain soon began to unravel. On 26 October 1605, Lord Monteagle, a member of the House of Commons, received an anonymous letter telling him to stay away from Parliament as something terrible was going to happen. Monteagle passed the letter to the authorities. On the evening of 4 November a search of the cellars below the chamber found Guy Fawkes, and his gunpowder.

On the morning of 5 November, when they realised that the plot had been discovered, most of the conspirators fled to the Midlands. As details emerged, the government ordered their arrest. Catesby persuaded his companions to continue with the second part of the plan and try to rally Catholics in England and Wales to join in the uprising, but no more than fifty people joined them and these soon melted away.

The king's men caught up with the conspirators on the morning of Friday, 8 November at Holbeche House in Staffordshire. There was a brief shoot-out and Catesby, together with three other conspirators, was killed. Two more were captured and brought to London. Sir Everard Digby was arrested over the next few days and was tried separately from the others on 27 January 1606. He was the only plotter to plead guilty. As he was a nobleman, he requested that he meet his end by the headsman's axe; this was refused. On 30 January he was dragged on a wattle hurdle to St Paul's Churchyard in London. There he mounted the scaffold and was stripped of his clothing. Murmuring, 'Oh Jesus, Jesus, save me,' he was hanged for a short period. Then the executioner cut the rope and Digby fell back to the scaffold, wounding his forehead. Fully conscious, he was taken to the block and castrated, disembowelled and finally quartered. His fellow plotters, including Fawkes, suffered the same fate. Even those who had perished at Holbeche House were exhumed and decapitated.

Woodcut showing the discovery of the barrels of gunpowder.

Ironically, even though Everard Digby had been executed for his attempted regicide, his son, Kenelm, who was born at Gayhurst in 1603, would in time become a great supporter of James I's son, King Charles I, during the Civil War. At the restoration in 1660 the Digbys were once again in royal favour, and the misdeeds of one of the thirteen Catholics who had tried to change the course of history were quietly forgotten.

AD 1642–1649

SKINHEADS V. LONGHAIRS

NO CIVIL WAR has cost Britain as many human lives as the English Civil War of 1642–1649. It was a conflict which pitted fathers, sons, brothers, cousins and friends against each other. It would devastate the country, destroy towns and homes, see an anointed monarch executed, and – for the first and only time in her history – turn England into a republic. Almost 200,000 people were killed, this at a time when the total population of the UK was estimated at only 5 million (of whom 2 million were eligible to fight). One in ten of the male population died – more than three times the proportion who perished in the First World War, and five times the proportion who died in the Second World War.

The war was the biggest military mobilisation in English history, with a quarter of those eligible to fight finding themselves in uniform. If the war had been fought today, with Britain's current population, the total number of dead would run into millions.

The causes and reasons for the war were complex, varied and longstanding. Fundamentally, it was due to the king's unyielding conviction that he was answerable not to his people or Parliament, but only to God. Another principle on which the war was fought was the king's arbitrary imposition of taxes, in particular the levy known as ship tax. This was traditionally imposed on coastal towns to pay for the upkeep of the navy, but in 1636 the king extended the tax to include inland areas, one of which was Buckinghamshire. One Buckinghamshire squire and landowner who saw the levying of ship tax as unconstitutional was John Hampden. As a Member of Parliament he represented Wendover and, in April 1640, was elected MP for the whole of the county. His refusal to pay ship tax on his land at Great Kimble and Stoke Mandeville put him at odds with the king. At Great Kimble church in 1636, he and other Buckinghamshire landowners declared their opposition to the levy. Hampden was singled out and subsequently put on trial and found guilty, though only by a slender majority: the narrow margin helped to undermine the king's absolute authority. It was Charles I's attempt to arrest Hampden – and five others – in the House of Commons in 1641 that ultimately plunged the country into civil war.

The war affected the whole country and Bucks was not to escape untouched. Although the main battles would take place elsewhere, Buckinghamshire would see its fair share of raids, skirmishes and sieges. Generally the county would come to side with Parliament, yet there were pockets of Royalist sympathy located at Buckingham, Winslow, Stony Stratford, Haddenham, and Brill. The hilltop village of Brill was in a difficult position. Aylesbury, only 14 miles distant, was occupied by Parliamentary troops from 1642 onwards. Oxfordshire, 12 miles away, on the other hand, was emphatically a Royalist county. Brill was therefore the centre of a sort of no-man's-land and, as such, the village was coveted by both sides.

John Hampden's statue in Aylesbury. His stand against ship tax hastened the events which led to the English Civil War.

John Hampden.

In December 1642 a Royalist force under the command of Sir Gilbert Gerard was sent to occupy Brill. However, in January 1643, Parliamentary troops were dispatched to dislodge the Royalists. The old castle earthworks surrounding the village had been developed into a defensive series of ramparts and ditches, which stood up well to the cannonade from the Roundhead force, and the assault continued off and on for 2 hours. The Royalists continued to hold out against the assault and the Parliamentarians eventually decided to withdraw. It was not until the winter of 1644 that Brill finally succumbed to the Roundheads.

Meanwhile, in November 1643, Olney, in the north of the county, was besieged by the king's dashing nephew, Prince Rupert. The town and surrounding area was held for Parliament, but the Royalists had surprised the Parliamentarians, forcing them to retreat to Olney Bridge. It was here that the townsfolk made a defiant stand, forcing the Cavaliers back. Rumours of reinforcements on their way from Newport Pagnell under the command of Cromwell convinced Rupert to withdraw.

One of the major incidents to take place in Buckinghamshire during the war was in November 1642 when Prince Rupert, in command of 10,000 horse and foot, attacked Aylesbury. The town was garrisoned by a small contingent of local militia whose numbers were no match for the Royalists, and the king's nephew entered without a fight. The townsfolk endured two or three days of plunder and despoilment as the cavaliers ran amok, before news came that a large Parliamentarian force, including John Hampden's regiment, was approaching to retake the town. Rupert decided to act first and rode out to engage the enemy. Both armies met at Holman's Bridge, just outside Aylesbury, with the Royalists charging the Roundhead infantry. The Parliamentarian centre was thrown back on to its lines of horse, whereupon a vicious struggle with sword, poleaxe and carbines ensued, both sets of troops slugging it out in a bloody throng. Rupert's men were eventually pushed back. The king's nephew tried to rally his soldiers but to no avail – a cavalry charge from the Roundheads sent them into a panic and they began to retreat back towards the town. Now it was the turn of the people of Aylesbury. Gathering what weapons they could, they rushed from the town and fell on the Royalist rear as Rupert's men fled for their lives back towards Thame. Townsfolk and soldiers now pursued the fleeing Cavaliers, cutting down stragglers. The chase continued for over a mile before the bloodshed ceased and the last of the king's army had got away. Hundreds of Royalists were killed for the price of only ninety roundheads. It was a victory against the odds, which might not have been achieved but for the folk of Aylesbury. It was also a sweet triumph for John Hampden: the king's forces had been defeated in the Buckinghamshire squire's home county. Yet it was a victory which was to be short-lived: seven months later Hampden would die at the Battle of Chalgrove in Oxfordshire.

Although the major battles of the war would decide its outcome, the conflict, in the main, would consist of raids on villages, towns and homes. In May 1643 the Royalists raided Winslow for arms and supplies. Buoyed by their success, they moved on to Great Horwood where

Prince Rupert of the Rhine. (With kind permission of the Thomas Fisher Rare Book Library, University of Toronto)

the villagers agreed to fork out £100 rather than be pillaged. Marching on to Swanbourne, they threatened to burn the village unless the inhabitants gave up their weapons. They refused, and Swanbourne was torched.

Despite this continual orgy of destruction, some soldiers found time for reflection. Sergeant Nehemiah Wharton marched from London with the Parliamentarian army to Worcester in August 1642. The route took them through Middlesex and Buckinghamshire. Uxbridge was ransacked, a poor unfortunate serving maid was shot dead by mistake and, on reaching Wendover, Wharton and his chums got drunk and smashed up the church. Still, the London sergeant found time to write home to tell his family, 'Buckinghamshire is the sweetest county I ever saw.'

Oliver Cromwell, the Lord Protector, who defeated King Charles I in the Civil War.

The south door of Hillesden church showing damage by musket fire.

Pastoral considerations aside, the war would continue to take its toll in lives, communities and families. In 1644 Sir Alexander Denton fortified his house at Hillesden, 5 miles from Buckingham, for the king and garrisoned it with 250 men. No less a person than Oliver Cromwell, together with the Governor of Newport Pagnell, Sir Samuel Luke, were ordered by Parliament to assault the house. The Roundheads, 2,000-men strong, attacked on the morning of 3 March 1644 and quickly overcame the defenders. Some retreated to the church and barricaded the doors, but these were soon broken in with musket fire, the scars of which can still be seen today. Within Hillesden house at the time of the siege were Denton's children, his sisters and nieces and members of the Verney Family from nearby Claydon. They were allowed to leave unharmed

He was a Chesham man, stood over 6 feet 7 inches tall, was a religious fanatic and from 1642 to 1649 served in the Parliamentarian army during the English Civil War. It is said he was sentenced to death by Cromwell for a breach of discipline and, while the sentence was never carried out, he received a blow on the head when in Colchester Prison. Thereafter his behaviour became somewhat strange. He led a life of celibacy and propounded the theory that it was sinful to eat flesh or fish or drink alcohol. He dressed in sackcloth, existed on 3 farthings a week and lived on a diet of dock leaves and grass. During his life he was imprisoned three times for witchcraft and was often put in the pillory or stocks.

Despite his odd behaviour he returned to Chesham and opened a hat shop. His enterprise was so successful that he became one of the town's richest men. In 1651 he sold his business, gave all his money to the poor and took to the life of a hermit, living in a hut in Ickenham near Uxbridge. He died aged 59, in 1680, forgotten and not mourned. His name was Roger Crab, and he may have been the inspiration for Lewis Carroll's creation 'the Mad Hatter', from *Alice's Adventures in Wonderland*.

In 1996, builders in Chesham unearthed part of a fifteenth-century building in the High Street, which is thought to be the site of Crab's hat shop.

by the Parliamentarians, yet several of the Royalist soldiers were shot, and Sir Alexander Denton and his offices were taken prisoner and marched to Padbury – where they were locked in the church for the night – before continuing their route to Aylesbury. Denton would never again see his beloved home. The house was burnt to the ground to prevent it falling into Royalist hands, and on New Year's Day, 1645, the Lord of Hillesden died in the Tower of London.

AD 1649

TO KILL
THE KING

ON A COLD, bleak day in January 1649, King Charles I stepped from a window in the banqueting house in London on to a 20ft-high wooden black-draped platform. A vast crowd of silent onlookers thronged Whitehall, anxious to gain the best vantage point to witness the final act in a bloody drama which had seen Britain plunged into a merciless eight-year civil war, and a king tried, found guilty and sentenced to death.

Charles I. (With kind permission of the Thomas Fisher Rare Book Library, University of Toronto)

Yet Charles I had in many ways forged his own path to the appointment with the executioner. His unshakable belief in the divine right of kings left the victorious Parliamentarians little choice; as Oliver Cromwell would remark on viewing the body of the king in his coffin, 'it [the king's execution] was cruel necessity.'

Following his defeat at the Battle of Naseby in 1645, and the subsequent discovery of correspondence proving that he was prepared to bring over Irish troops to fight for his cause, Charles was already in hot water. But who would kill the king?

Upon the scaffold also stood a block and a humble coffin in which the monarch's body would be placed. We may wonder if, in the king's last moments on earth, he considered those regicides who had brought him to this ignominious end. Perhaps one name to ponder was a Buckinghamshire man from the village of Dinton just outside Aylesbury. Simon Mayne was lord of the manor of Dinton and cousin to Oliver Cromwell. In 1645 he was elected MP for Aylesbury, and in 1649 was one of the judges who sentenced King Charles I

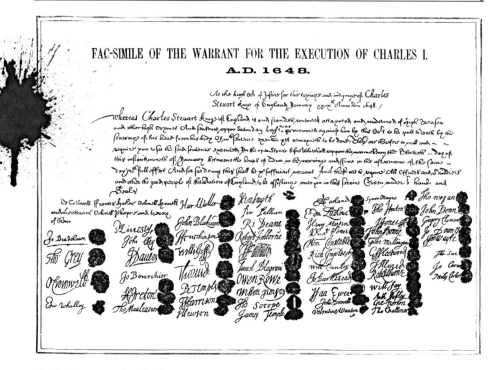

The death warrant for Charles I. Simon's signature can be seen at the top of the second column from the right.

to death. Mayne's signature was the fortieth out of fifty-nine on the king's death warrant.

At the restoration of Charles II in 1660, the Lord of Dinton fell from grace for his royal betrayal and was tried, sentenced to death and imprisoned in the Tower of London. He died before he reached the block, and his body was brought back to be buried in Dinton church.

THE DINTON HERMIT

There may have been another Buckinghamshire man who stood on the Whitehall scaffold with the king that day – someone who undoubtedly gained the monarch's attention. He stood with his face hidden by a leather mask; by his side was an axe, and he waited only for the doomed monarch to make his peace and place his neck on the block.

John Bigg was a native of Dinton who gained the sobriquet 'The Dinton Hermit' due to his choice of abode: a cave located somewhere in the village. It is believed to have been this Buckinghamshire oddity who brought the razor-sharp axe slicing down on to the king's neck and then held aloft the dripping royal head to show the crowd his grisly handiwork. The day after the execution, the monarch's head was sewn back on to his body and he was placed in a lead coffin. What became of Bigg is less clear, though it is thought that he returned to Dinton, where he was probably given sanctuary and anonymity by Sir Simon Mayne.

The head of Charles I as it appeared when it was exhumed in the Georgian era.

The history of the Hermit is veiled in mystery. It is thought that he had once been a medical student and a man of great learning, but following his master's demise he fell into a state of melancholy and betook himself to an underground cavern; here he hid himself away, shunning all company. He rarely strayed from his cave in the winter, though in the summer he sometimes frequented the woods around the village of Kimble, near Wendover. He lived the life of a recluse for many years, relying mainly on the kindness and generosity of the people of Dinton for his food and drink. His outfit was very singular: he begged for leather and cloth to patch and repair his ragged clothes and shoes, so over the years his attire became a patchwork. When he obtained a piece of leather, he patched the soles of his boots – eventually they became more than tenfold thickness. His dress included pantaloons which did not quite meet his shoes, a two-peaked hood, a short cloak and a belt from which hung three bottles: one for strong beer, one for small beer and one for milk.

Despite his unusual lifestyle, John Bigg lived to the respectable aged of 67 and was buried in Dinton churchyard. It has often been said that Bigg became a hermit because he was filled with remorse for his part in the death of the monarch. Following the restoration of Charles II, a commission was established to find those who had executed the king's father. Many eyewitnesses were questioned and several possible names put forward, yet no firm evidence was forthcoming as to the executioner's identity. Some believed it to have been the common hangman, as the grisly job of parting the Stuart king's head from his body had been rejected by those normally charged with such gory work. The one constant which emerged from the commissioner's investigations was that the executioner was a young man, no older than 20. John Bigg was born in 1629 – making him 20 at the time of the king's death.

AD 1665

A FUNERAL FRACAS IN AMERSHAM

SOMETIMES REAL LIFE has the ability to not only imitate comedy of the blackest kind but, in many cases, to surpass even the most absurd ideas. One such incident occurred in seventeenth-century Amersham.

In April 1665, the poet and author of *Paradise Lost*, John Milton, came to live in Buckinghamshire. At the time the plague was raging in London, claiming hundreds of people every week, and Milton, fearing for his life, asked his old friend and pupil Thomas Ellwood to find him a place to live in the area.

Ellwood, who was a Quaker, found the perfect 'pretty box', as he called the cottage, for Milton in Chalfont St Giles. There was great excitement at the prospect of the poet coming to live among his friends, and all was set for the day when he would be greeted at Chalfont. Unfortunately, it did not go according to plan.

On or near the day of Milton's arrival, Ellwood and a fellow Quaker, Isaac Pennington, were to attend the funeral of their friend, Edward Perot, in Amersham. Perot, an enthusiastic Quaker, had once travelled to Rome to try and persuade the Pope to ditch

Catholicism and become one of the Society of Friends. (He was soon on the return journey to England with a flea in his ear.)

The timing of the funeral was most inconvenient for Ellwood as there would be no one at the cottage in Chalfont to greet Milton when he arrived. Perot was a well-respected man in the area, and a good percentage of Quakers from the surrounding countryside were expected to attend his funeral. The day was set for 1 May, and Perot had specifi-cally asked to be buried in an orchard he owned at the other end of the town from his house, which meant the procession would make its way along the length of the High Street.

At that time, however, a certain Ambrose Bennet was passing through Amersham. Bennet was a barrister and Justice of the Peace. Unfortunately for Ellwood and his friends, the one thing which got right up Mr Bennet's nose was Quakers. He despised them. On hearing that a Quaker funeral was to pass through the town, Bennet and his men headed to the Griffin Inn where, joking and drinking, they planned to give Perot's cortège a boisterous welcome.

The Griffin Inn, Amersham, where local Quaker Edward Perot's funeral was rudely interrupted.

The coffin was taken up on to the shoulders of Perot's Quaker friends. Many mourners followed as they moved along the High Street, unaware of what was waiting for them at the Griffin. As the procession passed the inn, Bennet, his cronies and 'a rabble of rude fellows' rushed out and fell upon the funeral party. Bennet drew his sword and whacked the foremost bearer over the head, demanding he drop the coffin. The man refused to do so. This sent the drunken barrister into a raging fury and, grabbing the coffin from the bearers, he flung it to the ground. One can picture the scene: amid the screams, shouts and curses, Quakers and drunks grapple with poor Perot's coffin, swaying and tumbling all over the High Street. As if this wasn't enough of an outrage, the shocked and bewildered members of the funeral cortège who hadn't fled Bennet's drunken rogues were set upon and dragged into the inn.

While this unholy fracas was being played out in Amersham, back in peaceful Chalfont John Milton was wondering where his friends had got to; they were under guard at the Griffin, being abused and insulted whilst the unfortunate Perot, in his coffin, lay in the middle of the road. Carts went around him, horses avoided him, and people stepped over him.

Eventually a reluctant gravedigger was summoned and told to bury the coffin, without ceremony, in an unconsecrated part of the cemetery – much to Perot's widow's distress. Back in Chalfont, Milton still waited. At the Griffin, his friends were carted off to Aylesbury Gaol – although on what charge is unclear. Quakers are a peace-loving people; it's hard to picture them, in their sober black attire and wide buckle hats, having a punch up with a bunch of drunks in Amersham High Street.

Milton wouldn't see his old friends for some time: Ellwood and Pennington were locked up in Aylesbury for a month. On release, Ellwood went straight to Chalfont to see his friend. Milton was at the cottage, hard at work on his magnum opus, *Paradise Lost*. I wonder how the conversation went:

'Ah, Thomas, there you are. I was wondering where you'd got to!'

'Well John, it's like this. There was this funeral in Amersham ...'

AD 1690

IT'S THE END OF THE WORLD – EXCEPT FOR WATER STRATFORD

YOU MIGHT THINK that the phenomena of fanatical religious cults presided over by deluded, self-proclaimed Messiahs and followed unblinkingly by devoted converts seeking alternative spiritual enlightenment is a product of 1960s counterculture – yet such groups are nothing new.

The village of Water Stratford, 2 miles west of Buckingham, would seem to be the last place one would think of escaping to in the advent of a fiery Armageddon. Yet this sleepy Buckinghamshire backwater was, in 1690, besieged by a deluge of fanatical disciples convinced that it was the only place on earth which would be spared the ending of the world.

In 1674 John Mason became parish priest of St Giles at Water Stratford. He was a Puritan and was much admired by his fellow clergy. He wrote more than thirty hymns, including the still-popular *How Shall I Sing that Majesty*.

He was a man of gentle disposition and moderate views when he first took up his post. He was also said to harbour certain Calvinist sympathies; Calvinism was a religious doctrine formulated

by the sixteenth-century French theologian John Calvin, and one of its doctrines was that salvation is preordained and that God has already chosen those who are to be saved.

Mason and his wife lived happily at Water Stratford, administering spiritual guidance to his flock for some sixteen years, during which time he revealed himself to be a good and pious man. But then it began to go wrong. In 1690 Mason was hit by three successive personal blows: a scripture chronology he had worked on for years was rejected by the church authorities, and he grieved over his wasted time; secondly, his closest friend died; and finally, his beloved wife died. John Mason became a changed man; his grief was never to leave him. He began to experience strange dreams – nightmares and delusions that haunted his waking hours. They started to have an effect on his everyday life, and his preaching began to take on an alarming dimension. On Sunday mornings he would thunder forth from his pulpit that he was the prophet and miracle worker Elijah and that he could summon up the dead and bring down fire from heaven. He had been sent to Water Stratford to proclaim that the village had been chosen as holy ground, a place where the good and the privileged few could gather to await the day of destruction, whilst those outside this sacred boundary would be cast into the pit and destroyed by fire and sword.

Not surprisingly, Mason's superiors in the church began to get a little concerned. Not so his parishioners: the rector's congregation swelled as news of his message began to circulate. Hundreds of people from the surrounding area descended on the Buckinghamshire village eager to hear the word of the new Messiah. The crowds were so great that they packed into the churchyard to listen to Mason as he addressed the throng from one of the church windows.

Yet things were about to get even crazier. Hundreds of believers from miles around sold their property and moved to Water Stratford. They filled up the houses, barns and every place which could be used as accommodation. Some brought tents and pitched them on what they believed was the holy ground. They brought their livestock and mountains of food. Many were prepared to remain in this new Mount Zion until the day of judgement. They played musical instruments, and kept up a continual racket throughout the day and the night. There was singing, dancing and the frenzied clapping of hands. It seemed as if Water Stratford had gone mad. The population of the village was further increased by those of a non-religious persuasion, who turned

Water Stratford church, where hellfire preacher Revd John Mason addressed his devoted flock in 1690.

In 1705 a man named Browne Willis stood for election as MP for Buckingham. In those days election was not by universal suffrage, but by an electoral college presided over by thirteen burgesses of the town. Come voting day, only twelve of them were present: six voted for Willis and six for his opponent. 'Where is the thirteenth burgess?' the people asked. He was locked up in debtor's prison!

However, the poor man's fiscal situation was for the moment temporarily forgotten, and he was hastily released from his cell and asked to cast his vote. He did so – for Browne Willis – and was then just as quickly locked up again. It all seemed a bit of a waste of time, for although Willis represented Buckingham for three years he never once spoke in the House of Commons.

up to see what the fuss was all about. This was exacerbated when a third large group arrived, professing to be believers in the hope of receiving free bed and board. Clearly, the situation had grown out of hand.

Eventually the Church authorities, alarmed at what was happening, sent the Revd Maurice, Rector of Tyringham and a close friend of Revd Mason, to Water Stratford to report on what was happening. Maurice did not relish his task, and he set off for the village with more than a little apprehension. On his arrival he was welcomed by hordes of people dancing and chanting in loud voices. Inside the rectory he found a scene nothing short of pandemonium. Throughout the building, men, woman and children were running, climbing up and down the stairs, bellowing, laughing and clapping as if the Day of Judgment was just around the corner. Some were so overwhelmed with religious fervour and elation that they collapsed from sheer exhaustion. As they dropped to the floor, others took up the deafening frenzy.

Whilst Mason's followers danced themselves into euphoria, he lay in a garret at the top of the house. He was dying. He was being nursed by his sister, who warned Revd Maurice not to ask her brother anything about the scene downstairs. If he wanted to ask why Water Stratford had become the new Eden, he was to ask two of Mason's many disciples. Maurice was taken downstairs to talk with what Mason called his 'witnesses', but when he told them that he could not share their beliefs they became angry, telling him to be gone and to be damned.

Revd Mason died a month later. There were many at Water Stratford who were not sorry to see the demise of the firebrand rector, as it was hoped that his passing would put an end to the madness. However, it was not to be. Before he died, the rector had prophesied that he would return in three days, and the hordes remained in the village to see if it was true; the din of singing and chanting continued as they waited for Revd Mason to rise from his coffin. In desperation, Mason's successor, the Revd Rushworth, opened up the rector's grave and displayed the corpse, hoping to show one and all that their leader was indeed stone dead. Incredibly, however, there were still some who believed that the reverend would put in an appearance; the most stubborn hung around the churchyard for sixteen years, until eventually they were dispersed by the army.

The Church authorities put Revd Mason's weird behaviour down to smoking too much tobacco. It had obviously overheated his brain, and so kindled the zeal which brought about his end.

In early 1773 a rat-catcher and part-time chimney sweep by the name of Corbet broke into a house, accompanied by his dog, and murdered the tenant, Richard Holt. Corbet fled from the scene but inadvertently left his dog behind. When the authorities arrived to investigate the crime they had the best witness on hand to lead them to the killer: Corbet's dog, eager to get back to his master, led the pursuers straight to the murderer. Corbet was in possession of goods stolen from Holt; he was found guilty and sentenced to hang. He went to the gallows in Gib Lane, between Bireton and Hulcot, on a hot July day in 1773. And there his body, wrapped in iron bands, swung for the next twenty years, until finally only the skull remained.

THE WEIRDOES OF WEST WYCOMBE

WEST WYCOMBE LIES some 2½ miles from the centre of High Wycombe along the A40. It is a pleasing location, containing many fine half-timbered buildings dating from the fifteenth to eighteenth centuries; its church stands proudly on top of its ancient hill. However, this rural idyll was once the home of ghosts, murder, pagan worship and the debauchery of eighteenth-century titled gentry. Infamous activities are said to have taken place within the labyrinth of caves that snake their way beneath.

West Wycombe hill has been continuously occupied for thousands of years. A possible Bronze Age settlement, research has shown that a Pagan temple was constructed here in a similar style to Stonehenge. The Romans also built their own settlement and religious temple here.

During the Saxon period the site became the village of Haeferingdune (the hill of Haefer's people), a name which later evolved into Haveringdon. The hill retained its religious importance and the first Christian church was erected in AD 635. Haveringdon was greatly reduced by the Black Death in the fourteenth century, and by the early eighteenth century the village had relocated to the valley along the Oxford road. It was subsequently renamed, due to its position 'west' of the town of High Wycombe, with the villagers retaining St Lawrence as their parish church. Today no trace of Haveringdon village on the hill survives. With such an ancient and dark past, it seems appropriate that the one man who would become synonymous with West Wycombe took eagerly to the pleasures, rituals and rakish delights of eighteenth-century decadence.

In 1724, Sir Francis Dashwood (1708–1781), 2nd Baronet and later 15th Baron le Despencer, succeeded to West Wycombe park and set about building a house. Like many titled gentlemen of his day, he embarked on the grand tour of Europe and returned to England with his own grandiose plans for West Wycombe. The house, built, and added to between 1740 and 1800, was conceived as a pleasure palace for an eighteenth-century libertine. The building encapsulates the entire progression of British eighteenth-century architecture from Palladian to Neoclassical, and is set within a landscaped park containing temples and follies.

The baronet didn't limit his ideas and plans to just his home and gardens. In 1751 the fourteenth-century church of St Lawrence disappeared within Dashwood's rebuilding of the interior, modelled on the third-century Temple of the Sun at Palmyra in Damascus. Only the medieval tower was retained, which was considerably heightened and topped by a great golden ball fitted with benches, and large enough to contain six people. It was in the golden ball that Dashwood and his cronies drank the night away as they played cards and related bawdy stories. In 1765 the vast hexagonal Dashwood mausoleum was built east of the church. Its design was derived from the Constantine arch in Rome, and it was where the Dashwood memorials would be erected.

Yet, of all Sir Francis grand schemes for West Wycombe, perhaps the most ambitious was undertaken between 1748 and 1752 with the extension of a series of ancient chalk tunnels under West Wycombe hill into an elaborate labyrinth of caves and chambers. In order to provide work for the unemployed following a succession of harvest failures, Dashwood paid each labourer a shilling per day to excavate the passageways, which extended a third of a mile into the hill. Although it was a generous show of altruism, the baronet had other motives. The cave's design was inspired by Dashwood's travels in the Mediterranean. The descent through the passageways and underground chambers concluded by crossing a subterranean river named the Styx,

St Lawrence's church, West Wycombe. Members of the Hellfire Club met in the golden ball on top of the tower.

On 2 January 1736, Mr Pontifax, a Wycombe farmer, left the Antelope Inn in the centre of town after spending the evening with his sister-in-law, the landlady Mrs Haydon. At about midnight he made his way home towards West Wycombe, but a mile outside the town he was accosted by two 'rogues' who shot and robbed him. Pontifax was accompanied by his 13-year-old son who managed to escape the killers and raise the alarm. The murderers were arrested some weeks later at a London fair, and were tried at Aylesbury. Early on the morning of 22 March 1736, they were brought by cart from Aylesbury to the Rye Common in Wycombe and were executed on an extraordinarily high gibbet. Such was the frenzy of interest in the event that the whole of the town turned out to view the spectacle, pushing over the wall of the Royal Grammar School in the crush to see the two men hanged. The corpses were left to rot on the gibbet for four years before being cut down.

The Hellfire caves where Dashwood and his circle conducted their naughty rituals.

and entering into the inner temple, which is said to lie 300 feet directly below the church of St Lawrence. According to Greek mythology, the River Styx separated the mortal world from the immortal world, and the subterranean position of the Inner Temple directly beneath Saint Lawrence's church was supposed to signify Heaven and Hell.

Between 1750 and 1766 the Hellfire Club held their nefarious meetings in the caves below the hill. At first their drunken gatherings took place at the ruined Medmenham Abbey, situated on the banks of the River Thames, 8 miles south of West Wycombe. Here they called themselves the Monks of Medmenham, and their numbers

Could Granborough churchyard in the Vale of Aylesbury hold the grave of the oldest woman who ever lived? According to her gravestone she was born in 1491 and died in 1723 – at the age of 232! However, it seems that this lady's extraordinary longevity did not result from her taking regular exercise, eating a healthy diet or refraining from smoking. Her astonishing prolonged existence stems from the fact that the stonemason wasn't very good at his job, and made a mistake with his chisel. The good woman died at the age of 23.

included artist William Hogarth; political activist John Wilkes; John Montague, 4th Earl of Sandwich; poet Paul Whitehead and possibly, at times, future President Benjamin Franklin. It is uncertain what exactly the Hellfire Club members got up to during their twice-monthly meetings in the caves. They greeted each other as brothers and dressed as monks, while their accompanying ladies were attired as virginal nuns. Possibly some form of Satanic or pagan ritual mimicry took place, but more likely they indulged in drinking, gambling and whoring. The club disbanded amidst recriminations in 1766 following a practical jape played on the Earl of Sandwich during one of their drunken ceremonies – he believed that a monkey released from a box by a fellow member was the manifestation of the Devil, to much merriment from the group.

Following Dashwood's death in 1781 the caves fell out of use and became derelict. It was in the early nineteenth-century that the subterranean passageways and West Wycombe hill became the site of reported ghostly phenomena. When Paul Whitehead, a steward and secretary of the Hellfire Club and close friend to Sir Francis Dashwood, died, his heart was placed in an elegant marble urn in the mausoleum, as his will requested. In 1829 it was allegedly stolen by an Australian soldier.

AD 1750

SAD
SUKI

THE EIGHTEENTH-CENTURY George and Dragon pub in the village of West Wycombe stands on the old coaching route between London and Oxford. The locals and tourists who flock to its quaint half-timbered charm, keen to sample the ales and atmosphere, little know that the inn harbours a tragic tale – the story of the barmaid, Suki.

The George and Dragon inn, West Wycombe, which is haunted by Sad Suki.

Sixteen-year-old Suki, so the story goes, became infatuated with a handsome stranger passing through West Wycombe – much to the resentment of the local lads, who had their own designs on the pretty blonde barmaid. They sent her a message purporting to be from the handsome gentleman, instructing her to meet him in the caves at midnight. Dressed in her finest white dress she entered the caves, only to find that the message had been a hoax planned by the three jealous boys. In anger she threw rocks at the laughing lads. When the boys responded by throwing some back, Suki was knocked unconscious. Panicking, the local lads brought her unconscious body back to the George and laid her on her bed, where they hoped she would recover. Yet next morning her fellow servants found the beautiful young girl dead. Her ghost is said to walk the corridors of the George.

In 1967 an American tourist staying at the George was intrigued by the story of the ghostly barmaid and wanted to sleep in the haunted room. Part way through the night he awoke with a start as icy hands were placed on his forehead. When he turned on the lamp the feeling went away and the room was empty. Then he noticed a pinpoint of light near the door. As he watched it grew in length and width. It had a strange, opaque, pearly quality and would vanish when he switched the light on, only to reappear when he turned it off. Plucking up courage he went over to the light, but as soon as he reached it he felt the most intense cold; he couldn't breathe and his limbs felt heavy. Suddenly the illuminated form moved towards him and he leapt back in terror onto the bed, turning on the light as he did so. At once the strange shape vanished. The tourist slept no more that night and left early the next morning, vowing never to spend another second at the George.

The spectre of Suki has also been seen looking from the windows of the inn waiting and pining for her lost love. In the early 1990s the landlady of the George entered one of the rooms and saw the apparition of a young woman with a sad, lost expression sitting by the fire. After a few moments the ghost turned to look at the landlady and then slowly faded away.

The phantom barmaid is not the only ghost said to walk the rooms and corridors at the pub. Disembodied footsteps have been heard descending the main staircase and are believed to be the spirit of a visitor to the inn who was robbed and murdered in his room during the eighteenth century.

AD 1777–1878

'FETCH THE ENGINES, OLNEY IS ON FIRE ... AGAIN'

THOUGH OLNEY, IN the north of Buckinghamshire, is known as the birthplace of the famous pancake race, lace-making and hymn-writing, it surely must be the one location in the county never to reside without first taking out fire insurance. It would appear that over the years the town has suffered more than its fair share of conflagrations, some of which, it would seem, were not accidental.

The first was recorded in 1777 by the celebrated poet William Cowper, who was an Olney resident. Only seven or eight cottages were gutted, but if the wind had not suddenly changed direction half of the town would have been destroyed. Five years later another blaze almost consumed poor Olney. Cowper wrote again of an inferno that took place in November 1783. Being woken by screams of 'fire, fire', he looked from his bedroom window to see three fires raging across the town. It was thought that the fires had been started deliberately, and people frantically removed their furniture and possessions to places of safety. Cowper's own home became a temporary storage warehouse as Olney's panicking residents unloaded their belongings into his care.

Outside, throughout the smoke-filled streets, people were running this way and that in alarm. Chaos reigned and there was much drunkenness, looting and violence. Everything which was possible to steal was stolen and every drop of unguarded drink was drunk. In the mayhem George Griggs, who had rescued his life savings from his burning home, mistakenly gave the money to a woman he took to be his wife. The unknown woman, hardly able to believe her luck, took off through the blazing town and was never seen again.

Miraculously the fire did not claim any lives. Yet there were punishments to be meted out to those found to be looters, including many women who had filled their aprons with whatever they could lay their hands on and a young man convicted of stealing, who was sentenced to be horsewhipped through the town. However, the punishment descended into farce when it was discovered that the town beadle, whose job it was to administer the discipline, had a soft spot for the accused man and so had coated his hand with red ochre. After each stroke he drew the lash of the whip through the blood-coloured hand so it gave the impression that it was tearing the flesh from the young man's back, yet it was done in such a way as to cause no pain. The constable who was overseeing the punishment spotted the deceit and ordered the beadle to 'lay on with a will, or be struck in the same fashion'. But the charitable man would not do so and the procession continued through the town with the ridiculous spectacle of the beadle pretending to whip the young man, and the fuming constable caning the beadle. Eventually a female spectator, who could bear the ludicrous scene no longer, rushed forward and, grabbing the constable, punched him in the face. It is unclear if the incensed lady was made to join the whipping procession.

Yet only six years later, in 1786, another disastrous fire broke out, destroying forty-three houses. If the people of Olney had to live in fear of conflagrations being started accidentally, they also had the dread of those blazes ignited deliberately. Any moving shadow creeping through the dark streets at night could be someone intent upon arson.

In 1853 a number of local farms were deliberately torched. One cowshed was ignited with the animals still inside; the cries and bellowing of the terrified beasts was said to be unbearable to hear. The arsonists then started to target houses in the town, beginning with the bakery, whose flames quickly spread to a nearby watchmaker's. Two men, in an attempt to rescue their belongings from the burning building, were killed when the roof of the house came crashing down upon them. The fire-raisers continued with their deadly arson, and there was much

destruction of property in the town and surrounding area. It seems that the 'incendiaries' were intent on burning Olney to the ground. On 26 June 1854, whether by accident or design, that very thing almost happened.

Around 2 p.m. the most disastrous fire in the town's history broke out in the thatch-covered washhouse of a grocer's situated in the middle of the high street. The fire rapidly spread to a dyer's shop next door, and then the flames and burning thatch, carried on a boisterous wind, soon took hold of the blacksmith's and other buildings along the street. The blaze leapt from house to house – until dwellings, outbuildings, barns and farmyards were all engulfed in smoke.

The town's three fire engines, assisted by two from Newport Pagnell and one from Yardly Hastings, worked in vain with their manual pumps to douse the flames. But the relentless speed of the blaze could not be halted. It made its destructive way, leaping from building to building all along both sides of the high street. Ladders placed against the sides of the houses so people could remove their property were instantly consumed by flames. Those residents whose homes had not yet been reached by the fire tried to rescue their belongings before they were destroyed, but the unstoppable swiftness of the blaze overtook them. In all, almost eighty houses were destroyed, making more than 300 people homeless. Those who couldn't find shelter with friends or temporary accommodation in the town's unscathed premises were force to live in the open.

Despite yet another calamitous fire the Olney authorities seemed not to have learnt any lessons, for on the night of 3 January 1878, just over 100 years after the first conflagration broke out, the last straw was reached when Olney Mill caught fire. The town's fire engine arrived promptly on the scene, but there was little they could do to halt the rapid ferocity of the flames, which spread to the top floors and could be seen for several miles around.

Following the mill fire the people of Olney clubbed together to fund the first dedicated town fire brigade, consisting of twelve volunteer members who gave their time freely. Woe betide any fireman who didn't respond to the alarm; he was fined the astronomical sum of 10 shillings.

The Olney brigade was the pride of the town, and even though fires continued to break out the skill and organisation of the fireman prevented the conflagrations from spreading. Never again would Olney be subjected to the terror of an out-of-control blaze.

THE SCROOGE OF BUCKINGHAMSHIRE

HIS NAME WAS John Camden Neild. He stood no more than 5 feet high with an exceptionally large head, set upon a peculiarly short neck. His dress was shabby, with tight brown pantaloons, a ragged swallow-tail coat with gilt buttons worn over a filthy buff waistcoat and a dirty high-collared shirt with a large frill. His hessian shoes were patched and down at heel, and his stockings had seen far, far better days. In his hand he carried a mouldy green umbrella, and under no circumstance would he allow his clothes to be brushed, laundered or replaced – he thought this would shorten their life. One could well be forgiven for thinking that this quirky character, with his odd, jerky gait, walking along the highways and byways of Buckinghamshire, was a poor, penniless wretch down on his luck and on his way to the workhouse. But they would be wrong. For John Camden Neild was, by early nineteenth-century standards, a multi-millionaire.

He was born in 1780 in St James' Street in London, the son of James Neild, a sheriff of Buckinghamshire and a noted philanthropist, who liberally gave his time and money to service of the community. This was not the case with his son. The younger Neild was educated at Eton and Cambridge, where he studied law. He was called to the bar and it seemed he would pursue a career in the legal profession. However, in 1814, aged 34, he inherited his father's estates, worth £250,000, and all thoughts of becoming a barrister were abandoned for the more satisfying occupation of increasing and maintaining his wealth by unscrupulous, uncharitable or miserly means. By comparison he made Dickens' hook-nosed old skinflint Ebenezer Scrooge seem like a member of Oxfam. He lived in a large house in Chelsea, but it was so meanly furnished that for some time he chose to sleep on the floor of his bedroom rather than buy a bed.

He held property in Buckinghamshire, but preferred to walk from his London home to his estates to collect the rents from his tenants, rather than pay the coach fare. On the occasions when he did part with money for a journey to his tenants in Kent, he preferred to ride on top with the driver as the fare was cheaper, even though the weather was bitterly cold, with driving snow, and he wore no greatcoat. When the coach pulled into an inn so that the passengers might receive warmth and a hot toddy by a roaring fire, Neild preferred to remain outside on the coach in the freezing night. His fellow passengers, thinking the man somewhat embarrassed by lack of funds to join them, passed around a hat and sent him out a hot rum punch, for which he thanked them politely; then had the nerve to drink it down and remain on the coach.

When visiting his property he always stayed with his tenants, sharing their coarse meals and lodging. He employed a housekeeper who he paid a pittance, which was reduced even further when he was away from home as he calculated that she then did not do the same amount of work.

Why John Neild became a professed miser is unknown. He never married, and while at North Marston, in 1828, he attempted suicide by cutting his throat. His life was only saved by the prompt attention of his tenant's wife.

Owning property in North Marston, it was his duty to keep the church in a good state of repair. This he did, but reluctantly so. The roof of the church was in desperate need of renewal, but instead of using lead Neild went for the cheaper option of calico, saying 'it would see him out'. He remained on the roof all day long to ensure the workmen completed the job.

Even though he had amassed so much money, he only once felt the pang of philanthropy when he donated £5 to the building of a school and a whole £1 to the Sunday school at North Marston.

Balmoral, built with Neild's fortune. (LOC, LC-DIG-ppmsc-07532)

Apart from Bram Stoker's blood-sucking creation Count Dracula, perhaps the best known fictional monster in literature is Frankenstein, created by Mary Wollstonecraft Shelley in the early nineteenth century. In 1816, Shelley, together with her husband, the poet Percy Bysshe Shelley, and their friend John William Polidori, were holidaying on the shores of Lake Geneva at the rambling villa Diodati in Switzerland. During their stay the weather was particularly foul, with weeks of incessant downpours. Confined to the gloomy, rain-lashed villa, the companions were inspired to compose gruesome blood-curdling tales. It was Mary's composition, inspired by a nightmare, which proved to be the most disquieting, and it has since become a classic of Gothic horror.

Shelley's tale of the mad Victor Frankenstein and his monstrous creation would ultimately be the inspiration for numerous plays, books and almost 1,000 feature films. Two hundred years after its publication it still has the power to frighten and shock. Yet, even though the genesis of Frankenstein was conceived on the gloomily romantic shores of a Swiss lake, it was completed in the rather more mundane location of West Street, Marlow, in Buckinghamshire. When the Shelleys returned to England in 1816 they were encouraged to settle in Marlow by the writer Thomas Love Peacock, who would later write his gothic novel *Nightmare Abbey* in a nearby house. Marlow would appear to be a most appropriate location for the completion of Shelley's tale of an insane doctor: in 1758, until his death in 1776, William Battie, an eminent physician specialising in mental illness, lived in Court Garden House. The expression 'batty' is believed to have originated from his work with the mentally ill.

He died at No. 5 Cheyne Walk, Chelsea (Rolling Stone Keith Richards lived at No. 3 in 1966), on 30 August 1852, aged 72. Unloved and unmourned, he was buried in the chancel of North Marston church. His tenants attended the funeral but they came to watch, not grieve. One villager was heard to remark that if Neild had known how much it cost to bring his body from London to be buried in Marston churchyard he would have come down here to die.

Bizarrely, after a lifetime of miserliness he left the whole of his property, estimated at £500,000, to Queen Victoria, begging Her Majesty's most gracious acceptance. In 1855 Queen Victoria restored the chancel of North Marston church and inserted a window to Neild's memory. And then, with Neild's bequest, the monarch, who may have been amused, went off to build Balmoral Castle.

AD 1809–1814

THE VAMPIRE, THE PRESIDENT, AN EXILED KING AND THE TRAVEL AGENT

MANY OF BUCKINGHAM-SHIRE'S stately homes seem to have the most unlikely connections, and Hartwell House, just outside Aylesbury, is no exception. The property is first mentioned in Domesday Book of 1086 and was the estate of William Peveral, the son of William the Conqueror. It later belonged to John, Earl of Mortaigne (Evil King John of Robin Hood fame), who succeeded his brother Richard the Lionheart as King of England in 1115.

Although Hartwell dates back to Saxon times, the core of the present building was constructed in the seventeenth century for the Hampden family, and then the Lee family. The Lees were of ancient Buckinghamshire stock, and acquired Hartwell in 1650 by marriage into the Hampdens. Bizarrely, the Lee family tree includes not only American Civil War General Robert E. Lee and twelfth US President Zachary Taylor, but also British horror film actor Sir Christopher Lee.

Hartwell House.

Between 1809 and 1814 the owner of the house, Sir Charles Lee, let the mansion to the brother of the last king of France, King Louis XVIII. Following the French Revolution the monarchy was abolished in France and the king and his queen were forced into exile. The arrival of the impoverished monarch and his court at Hartwell was not a happy experience for the mansion. The once grand and haughty courtiers were reduced to farming chickens and assorted small livestock in the grounds and on the lead roofs. Louis was joined in his miserable exile at Hartwell by a collection of impoverished European royalty. His niece, the Duchesse D'Angoulême, daughter of Louis XVI and Marie Antoinette, and his brother, the Comte d'Artois (later Charles X), and Gustavus IV, the exiled King of Sweden, all had to make do with what the Buckinghamshire mansion could provide.

King Louis XVIII. He was proclaimed King of France in the library of Hartwell House.

Further unhappiness was to come on 13 November 1810, when the consort of King Louis, Marie Joséphine Louise of Savoy, died of dropsy at Hartwell at the age of 57. Her funeral was a magnificent occasion attended by all the members of the court-in-exile – whose names were recorded by police spies and reported back to Napoleon. The cortège was followed by the carriage of the British royal family, and Marie Joséphine was laid to rest in Westminster Abbey.

However, despite the queen's grand send-off, it was rumoured that the king had been repulsed by his wife, who was considered ugly, tedious and ignorant. The marriage remained unconsummated for years and, depending on which theory one believes, it was either due to Louis' impotence or his unwillingness to sleep with his wife due to her poor personal hygiene. She never brushed her teeth, plucked her eyebrows, bathed or used any perfumes. But he wasn't much to look at either. At the time of his marriage, the exiled monarch was so obese that he waddled instead of walked. He never exercised and continued to eat enormous amounts of food. The corridors of Hartwell not only creaked, but reeked.

Five years later, following the defeat of Napoleon at the Battle of Waterloo and the restoration of the monarchy, Louis XVIII proclaimed the Declaration of Hartwell. It was in the library that he signed the document accepting the French Crown. On his return to France for his coronation, he passed through Aylesbury with a great procession and Bourbon Street commemorates the king's royal line. However, it is thought that not all of Louis' court returned

The entry of the king and queen to Paris after the abdication of Napoleon. (LOC, LC-USZ61-1709)

with him to France. Many lie buried at Hartwell, and it is believed that descendants from members of his court are likely to live in Aylesbury and the surrounding countryside today.

In 1827, Dr John Lee, an astronomer, inherited the house and during his ownership the British Meteorological Society, now the Royal Metrological Society, was founded in the library in 1850. The telescope used at Hartwell observatory was designed by William Henry Smyth, whose daughter, Henrietta Grace, married the Revd Professor Baden-Powell. One of their children was Robert Baden-Powell who, in 1907, founded the Boy Scout movement. The house remained a private residence until 1938, when, at risk of demolition, the estate was acquired by the philanthropist Earnest Cook, the grandson of travel entrepreneur Thomas Cook.

Baden-Powell, whose great-grandfather designed the telescope used at Hartwell House. (LOC, LC-USZ62-96893)

THE MURDER OF NOBLE EDDEN

NOBLE EDDEN WAS a handsome young man. In 1828 he worked some land near Long Crendon, where he had established a small nursery and took his produce to sell every market day in Aylesbury. His land lay on high ground that commanded far-reaching views of the surrounding countryside. One day he caught sight of a movement in the fields below; two men were moving towards a flock of sheep. From the way they warily moved towards the animals, Edden knew they were up to no good. What's more, even from his distant vantage point the nursery worker recognised the two men. He was shocked, therefore, as he watched them move in among the sheep and proceed to kill one of the flock.

Soon afterwards the theft was discovered, and the area buzzed with speculation. Who had committed this crime? In 1828 sheep stealing was considered a most serious offence; it carried the death penalty or meant transportation. Noble Edden was well aware of this and he was torn: should he give up the men to the authorities or remain quiet? His word would have seen the men swing, and he didn't want their deaths on his conscience.

Curiously, despite his misgivings about reporting the theft, Eddens let the two culprits know what he had observed. Every time he met the men he looked at them knowingly and then commenced bleating like a sheep; 'Baa, Baa, Baa!' If he met them in the village, inn or on the road, it was 'Baa, Baa, Baa!' The two men ignored him, but they could hardly fail to realise that Edden knew of their crime, and that one word from him would be their end. Noble seemed to be ignorant or unconcerned about his own predicament, but men who are willing to steal, kill sheep, and are desperate to save themselves from the hangman are often also quite capable of silencing the one person who could put the rope around their neck.

One day, returning from Aylesbury market, Edden came across a man walking to Haddenham and he offered him a lift. The man recalled later that Noble had been in an agitated state and said he had a premonition that something terrible was going to happen to him. Meanwhile, back in the kitchen of their cottage, Mrs Edden suddenly had an awful feeling that something terrible had befallen her husband. In a vision she saw him being attacked by a man wielding a heavy hammer. She ran out into the street, crying out, 'Dear God, my husband is being murdered!' Her neighbours, alarmed at her distress, tried to calm her, but she insisted her vision was real. Noble Edden did not return home that night and later next day his body was found in a field near Haddenham. He had been beaten over the head, and his skull was crushed in.

At the inquest the following week, a verdict was returned of 'murder by persons unknown' and the body was returned to Mrs Edden. The moment the corpse was over the threshold, the distraught widow called for the man she had seen kill her husband in the vision – a man named Tyler – to come and lay his hand on the body. In those still-superstitious days, it was thought that if a murderer touched the body of

his victim the blood would flow from the corpse's mouth and ears and the face would change colour (hence the saying 'murder will out'). The accused refused the invitation.

Several months passed. Mrs Edden continued to insist that Tyler was the murderer, helped by an accomplice by the name of Sewell. Yet the two men could hardly be arrested on the evidence of Mrs Edden's vision.

During this time, Noble Edden's son took over his father's business. Returning from Aylesbury one dark night he was set upon by two rogues. The young Edden fought them off, but the two attackers were heard to say, 'We will do you the same as we did your old father.' It was too dark for the men's faces to be seen, but Noble's son recognised the voices as those of Tyler and Sewell.

Aylesbury Gaol. On 8 March 1830, 5,000 people gathered to watch the execution of the murderers of Noble Edden.

Just outside the village of Dinton, on the Aylesbury to Thame Road, stands what appears to be a ruined medieval castle. This is Dinton folly, and despite its ancient looking stone and crumbling masonry it dates only to 1769. It was built by the Lord of the Manor of Dinton, Sir John Van Hatten, to house his fossil collection. The structure was never completed as Sir John ran out of money. Tradition says the ghost of John Bigg, the Dinton Hermit and the supposed executioner of King Charles I, haunts the site. Other spirits may also well linger here, as evidence of an Anglo-Saxon burial ground has been unearthed.

On 16 August 1829, Sewell was arrested and charged with murder. He was committed to Aylesbury Gaol, where he made a statement implicating Tyler. Tyler was arrested three days later and both men were brought before magistrates. Mrs Edden related her account of seeing her husband murdered in a vision; she said that the man who had struck him was undoubtedly Tyler. Sewell's statement was then read out, in which he stated that he had seen Tyler strike Edden with the hammer. In rebuttal, Sewell's mother was called and was of the opinion that her son could not have been involved with such a terrible crime because he was an idiot. Imbecility ran in the family, and she had twenty-four children to prove it. Meanwhile Tyler continued to plead his innocence – and incredibly, the magistrate believed him. Sewell's evidence was considered unworthy and Tyler was released. The freed man went quickly home to Thame, dressed himself in gaily coloured ribbons and danced at the doors of everyone who had testified against him.

Sewell was brought before the court a week later and discharged (though the judge took the time to publically declare him a liar). However, the moment he stepped outside the court he was re-arrested for stealing a chicken and sent back to Aylesbury Gaol. He was sentenced to fourteen months' transportation, but in an attempt to save his skin he said he would at last speak the truth about the murder of Edden – Tyler was indeed the murderer, he claimed. But it didn't help him in his bid to be acquitted, and both men were sent to trial. Sewell played the idiot whilst in the dock, repeatedly waving to the gallery, and Tyler declared that he was 'as innocent as a new-born baby'. Yet both were found guilty of Noble Edden's murder.

On 8 March 1830, 5,000 people gathered outside Aylesbury Gaol to witness the execution. Sewell kept up his imbecilic games, calling out goodbye to the crowd, 'I am about to die and go to heaven.' Tyler trembled with fear and declared his innocence. Before he could say any more, caps were drawn over both men's faces and the next moment the trapdoor opened.

AD 1832–1849

THE SCOURGE OF CHOLERA

THE TERM 'TRUTH IS stranger than fiction' is often applied to those incidents and episodes which leave the reader scratching their head in disbelief. The following account demonstrates this only too well.

One morning in 1832, a resident of Marlow said goodbye to his wife as he went off to work. He told her he would return that evening and that they would enjoy a good dinner together. The man's wife was happy, healthy and in good spirits as she bade farewell to her husband. However, when the man returned that evening he was surprised to find the house empty and his wife not at home. Soon, distraught and anxious, neighbours came to the man's home to tell him the devastating news that his wife had died that morning, and had to be hurriedly buried.

The distressed man could not believe that his true love had been taken from him so quickly and without warning. In anguish he rushed to the churchyard where she had been laid and desperately dug down to the coffin and opened the lid. To his astonishment he perceived signs of life, which were soon confirmed when the woman sat

Statue group representing the city of Paris (the woman) pleading for God to take away the scourge of cholera (the old, dying man and the sick child). (LOC, LC-USZ62-31215)

up in the coffin, to the great joy of her husband. The woman recovered and both returned home, much to the amazement of the locals. Incredibly, that same night, the woman gave birth to a child.

One word lurks behind this astonishing story: cholera. In 1818 reports of an appalling disease reached England. Once contracted, death could occur in days, and sometimes hours. Symptoms began with diarrhoea, vomiting and agonising pains in the limbs and stomach. Fever and dehydration soon followed, with the victim's eyes becoming sunken and the skin and hands wrinkled. Eventually seizures occurred and the person descended into a coma.

Cholera has its origins in the Indian subcontinent where it was ravaging the population (and killing the British soldiers who were stationed there). By 1830 it had reached Russia and the Baltic ports, spreading so rapidly that by the time it reached Britain in 1831, there was almost 4,000 cases and 900 deaths. The people of Buckinghamshire were terrified and wondered when the scourge would arrive in their neighbourhood. They didn't have to wait long. In June 1832 cholera appeared in Aylesbury, with fifteen cases and five deaths. Those who perished had to be buried quickly to prevent the disease's spread and midnight funerals, under the cold glow of a solitary lantern and with no mourners to watch the coffin hastily covered with earth, were commonplace.

Within a week there were an additional 141 cases in the town, fifteen of them fatal. By 15 July a total of fifty people had perished and in October the disease had been reported in Chesham, where eight residents died.

Knowledge of how it was started or carried was unknown, though it is now believed that poor sanitation was to blame. Disease-ridden slums, especially those in the cities, allowed cholera to freely flourish. Many villages and towns were without adequate water supplies, sewerage systems or refuse collection. If the streets and drains stank it was put down to bad weather and in Aylesbury pigs roamed the streets eating the refuse. As always, the poorer sections of society were hit the hardest.

The authorities were at first berated and then implored to do something, though no one wanted to be called upon to pay extra for the habitation of the poor. Yet it soon became apparent that if the disease was allowed to thrive in the hovels of poorest it would soon find its way to the homes of the richest. Aylesbury was thought to be a perfect breeding ground for cholera: a town besieged with mephitic vapours, its outskirts poisoned by putrid ditches and obstructed by narrow channels dismissively called drains. An Aylesbury resident and hero of those affected by the scourge, Dr Robert Ceely, declared that the sanitation for the poor of the town was a disgrace to civilisation. The majority of the town leaders were not pleased with the findings of the doctor and were disinclined to fork out extra rates to help the poor.

By August 1832 the disease appeared to be on the wane. Although many people in Buckinghamshire had died from the scourge, the county seems to have got off comparatively lightly as throughout Britain some 30,000 had perished from cholera. Yet it was not the last the people of Buckinghamshire would see of this modern-day plague.

In 1848 another epidemic broke out worldwide and soon people in the

Aylesbury County Hall was built in 1740, and was the scene of public executions for over 100 years. One of these was a young man by the name of Constable who was sentenced to hang for sheep-stealing. After he had 'dropped', his mother brought his body back to Stony Stratford for burial. The poor dead man's mum couldn't have been too distraught at her son's demise, though, for before the interment she put the body on show at Stony fair and charged a penny a peep.

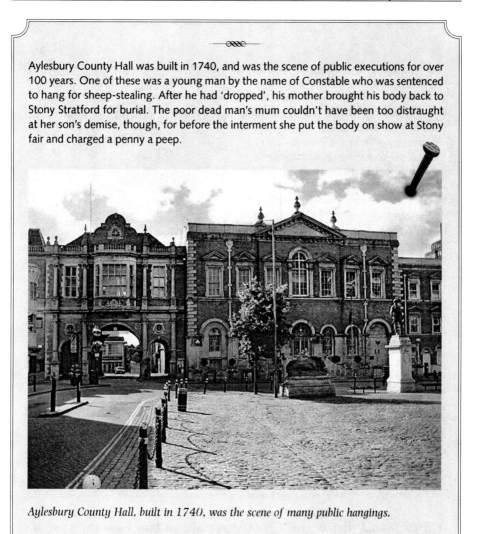

Aylesbury County Hall, built in 1740, was the scene of many public hangings.

towns and villages of Buckinghamshire were dropping like flies. The disease had been reported at Wycombe, Marlow and Chesham and flight from the overcrowded urban slums was ineffectual at escaping the illness. In August 1849, at the oddly named rural hamlet of Gibraltar, just outside Aylesbury, seventeen deaths were reported. By the time the disease had begun to decline forty-eight people had died, from a population of just fifty-five. Tragically for the people of Gibraltar, history was repeating itself: during the Great Plague of 1665 a sizeable group of Londoners made their way to the hamlet to escape the disease, as one of their number had a relative in the village. They unknowingly brought the illness with them, resulting in forty people dying.

American author and anglophile Bill Bryson once observed that it was impossible to walk a mile in Britain without coming across some fascinating historical fact or interesting curiosity. He was, of course, quite right.

The village of Penn near Beaconsfield in the south of the county is a good example of an ordinary Buckinghamshire location with some extraordinary connections. William Penn, founder of the city of Philadelphia in the USA and after whom the state of Pennsylvania takes its name, claimed the village of Penn as his ancestral home. His sons lie within the church crypt, and Sir William, his wife and his family lie in nearby Jordan's churchyard.

Penn church is also the last resting place of David Blakeley. He was murdered by Ruth Ellis, the last woman to be hanged in Britain. Her grave is in nearby Amersham churchyard. Penn church also contains the graves of the parents of spy Donald MacLean. He, along with Guy Burgess and Kim Philby, betrayed Britain's military secrets to the Soviet Union just after the Second World War. On discovery, all three defected to Russia. When MacLean died in 1983, his will requested that his ashes be returned to England and scattered on his parents' graves. Other former residents of Penn include the actor Stanley Holloway, poet Walter de la Mare, and Louisa Garrett Anderson, the first woman in Britain to qualify as a doctor.

William Penn. (LOC, LC-USZ62-106735)

It is estimated that up to 90,000 people died of cholera in Britain during the worst outbreaks. Those who survived the foul infection were lucky. Even more so were those who were infected, wrongly presumed dead and buried with frightful haste, only to reveal that they were still alive at the last moment. Many may not have been so lucky: as the coffin lid was hammered down they lay, still conscious, and in the blackness of their wooden tomb, listening to the sound of earth filling in their grave.

MURDER, BUCKINGHAMSHIRE STYLE

THERE ARE MANY words to define a murder: horrific, cruel, brutal, vicious ... Yet for the three barbaric killings described below, one could also employ the terms insane and downright idiotic.

The Ostrich Inn, Colnbrook, dates back to the eleventh century. It is thought to be the third-oldest public house in England, and was used as a resting point for travellers on the road between London and Bath. However, a night at the inn could prove to be a very dangerous experience.

During the seventeenth century, a landlord of the Ostrich by the name of Jarman decided to relieve some of his more wealthy clients of the large sums of money they were carrying following their return from doing business

The Ostrich Inn, Colnbrook.

in London. One might have thought the easiest way for the landlord to carry out his plan was to simply creep into the unsuspecting guest's room after they had been rendered unconscious by too much drink and help himself to their bulging purses, then assign the blame to unscrupulous guests staying at the inn. But that was too simple for Jarman. With echoes of the Demon Barber, Sweeney Todd, and his method of murderous dispatch, the devious landlord installed a large trapdoor under the bed in the best bedroom, located immediately above the inn's kitchen. The bed was fixed to the trapdoor and the mattress securely attached to the bedstead, so that when two retaining iron pins were removed from below, in the small hours of the morning, the snoring guest was neatly dropped into a boiling cauldron. Jarman and his wife killed more than sixty of their richest guests in this barbaric fashion. The scalded corpses were then disposed of in the River Colne.

The murder of a wealthy clothier proved to be Jarman's undoing, for he failed to get rid of the guest's horse. This led to the suspicion that the unfortunate man was still somewhere, dead or alive, within the inn. The landlord and his wife tried to flee Colnbrook once they were discovered, but were appended in Windsor and swiftly tried, convicted and hanged for robbery and murder.

THE DENHAM MASSACRE

In 1870 at Denham, in the south of Buckinghamshire, a no-less barbaric set of murders took place which saw an entire family bludgeoned to death.

On 22 May of that year, 38-year-old John Owens, a Wolverhampton-born drifter, gained entry to the home of Emanuel Marshall, the village blacksmith, and beat to death everyone inside. Owens bore a grudge against the blacksmith, believing that he was being paid an unfair wage. Prior to the murders, the drifter had served a prison sentence for petty crimes, but on release made his way to Denham hell-bent on bloodshed.

First to die was Emanuel Marshall, struck over the head with a sledgehammer. Next was the blacksmith's wife, cut down by an axe Owens had taken from the smithy. Her sister, who was woken by the bloodcurdling screams, was also hit with the bloody cleaver. It seems that Owens had now gone completely insane, for he next murdered Marshall's 77-year-old mother. Yet the horror had not ceased, for the crazed killer then cut down the three Marshall children, aged 8, 6, and 4.

With his bloodlust satiated, Owens fled the house. But he was seen leaving and later, following the discovery of the horrific killings, was arrested at Reading.

He was tried and sentenced to death. Two days before his execution he asked if he could spend his last nights on earth in the coffin he was to be buried in. It is unclear if his request was granted. On the morning of his execution he threatened to beat up the hangman for not having the courtesy to visit him in his cell the previous day. He went to the gallows at Aylesbury on 8 August 1870, and perhaps few men were more deserving of the drop than he.

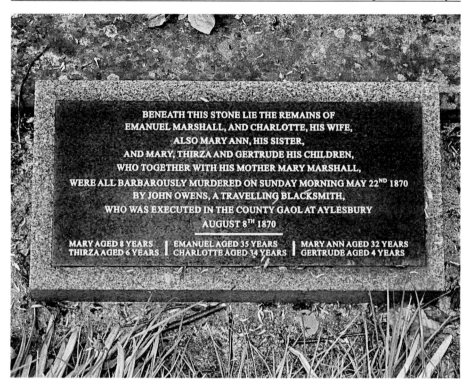

BENEATH THIS STONE LIE THE REMAINS OF
EMANUEL MARSHALL, AND CHARLOTTE, HIS WIFE,
ALSO MARY ANN, HIS SISTER,
AND MARY, THIRZA AND GERTRUDE HIS CHILDREN,
WHO TOGETHER WITH HIS MOTHER MARY MARSHALL,
WERE ALL BARBAROUSLY MURDERED ON SUNDAY MORNING MAY 22ND 1870
BY JOHN OWENS, A TRAVELLING BLACKSMITH,
WHO WAS EXECUTED IN THE COUNTY GAOL AT AYLESBURY
AUGUST 8TH 1870

| MARY AGED 8 YEARS | EMANUEL AGED 35 YEARS | MARY ANN AGED 32 YEARS |
| THIRZA AGED 6 YEARS | CHARLOTTE AGED 34 YEARS | GERTRUDE AGED 4 YEARS |

The grave of the Marshall family in Denham churchyard.

MURDER AT THE FARM

It was shortly before midnight on 1 November 1853 that Ralph Goodwin returned to his farm at Burnham after visiting friends. Goodwin employed several people in his house and on the farm, and two of these were his housekeeper, Mary Sturgeon, and a 23-year-old groom and servant by the name of Moses Hatto. Sturgeon and Hatto disliked each other intensely, but the young man would have to hold his tongue in any dispute, as the housemaid's services were valued more highly by the master of the house.

On the night in question, Goodwin had instructed Hatto to wait up for him to stable his horse on his return. Yet as soon as the farmer entered the house he noticed something odd. The young man appeared edgy and his demeanour was strange.

Hatto informed his master that an hour earlier he had heard noises in the yard and he and another worker, John Bunce, had gone to investigate. A colt had got free and the two men had tried to catch it. The groom told his master that he had called up to Mary Sturgeon's bedroom window for her to come and assist, but there was no reply from the housekeeper.

As Goodwin entered the kitchen he noticed spots of blood on the door and on the floor matting. When he asked Hatto how they had got there, the groom just shrugged his shoulders and said he didn't know. The farmer also discovered a tooth and a bloody hairpin on the kitchen floor. Feeling sure that something was amiss, Goodwin went to find his housekeeper. On reaching the landing he saw smoke coming from Mary Sturgeon's bedroom. He at once raised the alarm and called for Hatto to fetch water. On entering, they found the room on fire and several buckets were needed to extinguish the flames.

As the smoke cleared Goodwin saw the body of the housekeeper lying on the floor in a pitiful state. Her legs had been badly burned, whilst the clothes covering her body had been singed. A doctor soon reported that the housekeeper had been beaten to death with a heavy implement. Suspicion immediately fell on Hatto and blood found on his clothing further implicated him. He was charged with Mary Sturgeon's murder and, despite at first pleading his innocence, he eventually admitted his crime. He had attacked the housekeeper in the kitchen with a lard beater, and then, when she fled in terror to her bedroom, he pursued her and beat her to death with a poker. In an attempt to conceal his crime he tried to burn the body. This we may view as idiocy of the first kind. Did it not occur to Hatto that to set fire to a body in a bedroom mostly constructed of wood meant a pretty good chance of the rest of the building going up in flames?

Moses Hatto was the first man to be hanged outside the new Aylesbury Gaol in Bireton Road, on the morning of 24 March 1854.

FLYING SAUCERS OVER HIGH WYCOMBE

THE NOTION THAT extra-terrestrial life exists somewhere in the unfathomable vastness of the universe is often viewed by scientists with derision and by sceptics with ridicule. However, consider that 'out there' in space are 100 million galaxies, each containing a billion stars, around which a jaw-dropping 1,000 billion trillion planets orbit. Given such eye-watering statistics, can we really say we are alone in the universe? It would seem that one person who was convinced that E.T. is definitely out there was a High Wycombe businessman by the name of William Robert Loosley. He witnessed 'denizens from another world' – or did he?

One night in October 1871, Loosley was in his garden to get some fresh air after waking with a slight fever. The time was 3 a.m., and on looking at the sky he saw what he thought was a star falling to earth with a great roar. In shock, he realised that the plummeting light was not a star but some kind of craft whose trajectory would bring it down on Plomer hill in Downley, west of the town centre.

The craft disappeared from sight within the dark folds of the hills, but Loosley did not hear any sound of an impact. The following day he set out to find evidence of the object that surely must have crashed to earth. On reaching the site, Loosley found no sign of debris or evidence of any resulting fire, but did discover two unusually shaped metal objects that moved by themselves and made whizzing and whirring sounds. They shone purple lights into his eyes, whereupon he could see amazing futuristic visions, including ghostly images of himself. Terrified, he fled the scene. He felt compelled to write down an account of the incident but was also aware that if knowledge of what he saw was made public he would be ridiculed, so he decided to hide his written account of what we would today call a UFO in a secret drawer of a desk.

And there it lay for a century before it was discovered by his great-great-granddaughter, Edith Salter. Mrs Salter passed the written account of the UFO on to the science journalist and sci-fi writer David Frankland, who was given permission to publish it in a book he was writing on flying saucers.

On an August Bank Holiday in 1891 all of High Wycombe was in a state of high excitement when it was announced that the daredevil Professor Higgins, accompanied by his lovely assistant Miss De Voy, the renowned parachutists, were to ascend in a gas balloon to an astonishing height above the town, whereupon they would leap off and descend safely back to earth by parachute. The professor was an old hand at this exceptional feat of daring: he once parachuted from a balloon 12,000 feet above Wolverhampton and survived.

The Wycombe take off and jump was scheduled for 6 p.m. from Loake's meadow and vast crowds had gathered to watch the two intrepid flyers ascend. But it didn't go according to plan. Once filled with gas, the balloon went sideways instead of skywards, scattering the crowd as it scraped and brushed along the floor. Miss De Voy, sensing that she would get no higher than the treetops, leapt from the balloon as it climbed pathetically upwards. It passed over the western end of town until it came down to earth coughing, spluttering and deflated in a field.

Who was to blame for the balloon's dismal performance? The parachutists accused the gas company of filling the balloon with inferior gas. The gas company accused the flyers of having a second-rate craft that let the gas seep out, as almost 70,000 feet of good quality gas had been pumped into the balloon. Either way, all were disappointed, especially the Wycombe crowd who – with great restraint – refrained from showing the failed jumpers what they thought of them.

A week later the professor and Miss De Voy were offered the chance to redeem themselves, with the incentive of £30 if they completed the jump. However, only a few days before, at Paignton in Devon, another parachuting professor was almost lynched when his planned jump failed to get off the ground. Similarly, in Nottingham 5,000 spectators, having been kept waiting for over 2 hours, went berserk when another parachute jump failed to happen. They tore up the balloon and mobbed the police station where the terrified parachutist was hiding.

Bearing this in mind, the professor and Miss De Voy thought better of risking their lives to a baying mob if things didn't go according to plan and, with their faulty balloon, quietly slipped away from Wycombe.

What was to be done? The crowd still wanted to see someone leap from a balloon over the town. Step forward 19-year-old Cissi Kent, pretty as a picture and without an ounce of fear. The ascent was planned to take off from the Wycombe gas works and a vast crowd gathered, including the mayor and council dignitaries. Members of the fire brigade held the balloon, and were on standby in case a stray cigar ember found its way to the gas and gave Wycombe its own version of the Hindenburg disaster. Miss Kent took up position, clad in a blue velvet knickerbocker suit, cap and light pink stockings. At 5.30 p.m., after a dinner of soup, lamb cutlets, plum pudding and a bottle of claret, the cheering crowds watched as she lifted off into the air. A slight breeze got up and carried Miss Kent along the Wycombe valley, where her balloon rose to the astonishing height of 6,000 feet above the Rye. Soon the white mushroom of her parachute could be seen drifting slowly down to earth where it landed safely in a barley field near the Rifle Butts pub. There were cheers all round and everyone concerned repaired to the Red Lion inn, where they stayed for the rest of the evening. The balloon made its way to Surrey, where it crash-landed in a cornfield.

Frankland was wary, almost as much as Loosley, that the account of the UFO would be debunked as the madness of a crank. He needn't have worried, for when the book was published in 1979 Loosley's story entered into UFO lore as an amazing and detailed account of what could only be explained as an alien visitation. And yet the truth is that the whole story was a fraud perpetrated by Frankland as a practical joke, played on believers and lovers of UFOs.

What is fascinating about Frankland's hoodwink is that he chose an obscure High Wycombe businessman as central to his charade. He acknowledges Loosley's granddaughter for her help, and also includes photos from the 1880s of Loosley's grave in Wycombe cemetery and his shop on Oxford road, to lend substance to his story. Strangely, the incident is still considered by uninformed authors as a true, first-hand account of a UFO sighting.

Frankland's hoax is not unique. In 1970, journalist Frank Smyth set out to see if he could invent a ghost, and what response it would generate. He therefore created the mad vicar of Ratcliffe Wharf in London. Smyth's story claimed that an eighteenth-century clergyman from St Anne's church on the Isle of Dogs, who owned a boarding house in the area, was in the habit of murdering his guests, robbing them and dropping their bodies into the Thames. It goes on to claim that the vicar was apprehended and executed, and since then his ghost has been reported walking the streets of Limehouse. Incredibly, the story quickly became East-End folklore, with people claiming to have seen the ghost, and within a year eight separate books had been written about the fictitious phantom, some even embellishing the story with added details. Smyth eventually admitted the deception and sightings of the vicar ceased. Likewise, up to the present no reports of Unidentified Flying Objects have been reported over High Wycombe.

AD 1891

THE CHILTERN MANHUNT

ON THE MORNING of Sunday, 13 December 1891, two bodies were discovered in woodland on the Ashridge estate near the village of Pitstone, only 150 yards within the county boundary of Buckinghamshire on the Hertfordshire border. They were William Puddephat, a gamekeeper, and Joseph Crawley, a nightwatchman. Both had been battered to death and had lain in the open all night before being discovered by the head keeper. Beside one of the bodies was part of a broken gun, which had been the weapon used to fell Crawley. Footprints at the scene revealed that Puddephat had tried to run for his life before he was pursued and struck down. Further examination of the area revealed tracks that headed away from the crime scene, across fields towards the village of Ivinghoe.

It was quickly established that the men were the victims of a bungled poaching expedition. The night before the murders had been perfect for poaching: windy and bracing, with the trees being whipped this way and that, and the full moon shining and peeping intermittently behind racing clouds.

Suspicion immediately fell on three habitual poachers from Tring in Hertfordshire, who had been witnessed near the crime scene on that tempestuous night. Their names were Eggleton, Rayner and Smith and there was no doubt locally that these were the guilty men. However, Smith, on realising that Eggleton and Rayner were intent upon murder, had run for home. Early next morning, Eggleton and Rayner called at Smith's home saying the game was up and they all had to go on the run; Smith's wife told them to clear off otherwise she would call the police. Poachers were normally the local heroes when it came to taking the odd bit of game or wild animal from the lord of the manor's estate, but this was murder and the whole countryside waited for the killers to be caught.

The two culprits immediately took to their heels and headed for nearby woodlands. Eggleton and Rayner were soon pursued all over the Chilterns in one of the biggest manhunts in nineteenth-century Buckinghamshire.

First sightings of the men were reported at Tring as they tried to purchase food. Soon the scene switched to Wendover, when a shepherd observed two men behaving in a sneaky manner as they emerged from woodland on a hill; realising they had been seen, they ducked back into the cover of the trees. The bulk of the Buckinghamshire constabulary rushed to Wendover, leaving only two constables in Aylesbury to police the town.

Assisted by local beaters, the police entered the woods in an attempt to drive the men from their cover, and several times came close upon the two or heard them only a short distance away. Yet the two fugitives were adept at evasive action and they managed to escape the pursuing police.

They were next sighted in High Wycombe, but were soon chased into Oxfordshire. Here the two went under-cover, obtaining threshing work on a farm. They were recognised and arrested by the Oxon police, who promptly measured them. However, as their heights did not conform to the official figures, the two men were released. Yet the arresting constable was convinced that they were the guilty men and he returned to the farm. Eggleton and Rayner spotted the policeman coming and hastily headed back to Buckinghamshire. The officer was determined to catch his fugitives and gave chase, but the men were getting away from him. The policeman thought about giving up the pursuit when he spotted a pony in a field. Throwing off his helmet and tunic, he quickly mounted the (no-doubt astonished) beast and both set off after the killer poachers. For 12 miles pony, policeman and breathless poachers scampered across the fields in a desperate chase.

However, it was all too much for the poor animal and he ultimately broke down, exhausted, leaving the sore-bottomed officer to watch as the two men crossed over the border into Buckinghamshire.

They were next seen back in High Wycombe, but soon the chase moved to Great and Little Missenden, where they were spotted purchasing food at the Nag's Head on the Amersham road. Further reports said that they had doubled back to Prestwood. Yet a few days later, Chesham was being scoured for the desperate escapees. It wasn't long before the men were sighted in Amersham, Beaconsfield and Slough. So many sighting were being reported that the situation was beginning to become farcical.

In Denham the two men were seen entering a public house to sell a knife in exchange for food. Soon the whole area was swarming with police – but once again the murderers managed to elude their pursuers, and made for a farm to hide themselves away until the coast was clear.

Just over a week after the murder of the two gamekeepers, Eggleton and Rayner emerged from their hiding place, thinking that the police had gone. But they were immediately arrested and taken at first to Slough and then by train to Aylesbury. The capture of the killers generated great excitement in the area, and the two men's destination had to be kept secret to avoid a mob forming. However, when the train conveying the men stopped at High Wycombe and Princes Risborough, it was besieged by angry mobs. At Aylesbury they were met by several hundred demonstrators and had to be bundled out of the train and taken, for their safety, to a police station, pursued all the way by a shouting and hooting crowd. After eight days and nights running from the law, the two terrified men were thankful to be in police custody.

Smith had been arrested some days earlier, and the trial of the three men took place at the end of February 1892. All three were charged with murder. Each sought to blame the other for the crime: Eggleton stated that he had been struck on the head by one of the gamekeepers, and was unconscious when the killing had taken place; Rayner said that *he* had been rendered unconscious, and added the horrific detail that Eggleton had told him he'd put his fingers into one of the victims'

smashed-open brains to confirm he was dead. Their accounts fell on deaf ears: both were found guilty and sentenced to death. Smith was found guilty of manslaughter and sentenced to twenty years' hard labour.

Eggleton and Rayner went to the gallows protesting their innocence, and were hanged at Oxford Gaol on 17 March 1892. Between them the three offenders had three wives and fifteen children. The murdered men's dependants numbered two wives and twelve children. Four men dead and thirty-two people unprovided for – and all for the sake of a few pheasants! The total is made all the more tragic when, from his death bed after eighteen years of incarceration, Smith reputedly confessed to murdering both men ...

AD 1890s

THE STAB MONKS OF CHALVEY

SOME BUCKINGHAMSHIRE TOWNS have quaint customs when it comes to how they view and choose their respective mayors. In High Wycombe the prospective candidate is weighed, as is the outgoing mayor, along with the councillors and officials. If it is found that they have gained in pounds during their term in office they are greeted with jeers and boos. If none of the town's dignitaries have gained weight by benefiting from their official posts they are roundly cheered by the people.

However, there is one Buckinghamshire town where successful mayoral candidates don't need to watch the pounds to be approved by the townsfolk; instead, to become Mayor of Chalvey, one has to be stone-dead drunk. But how did this rather odd, but nonetheless pleasant, mayoral election process come about?

In the middle to late nineteenth century, Chalvey, near Slough, had an unusual attitude towards pets. In an unspecified year in the late 1800s, an Italian organ grinder was performing with his pet monkey in the village when a young child, keen to get near to the colourfully dressed baby ape, came too close; it was rewarded with a vicious bite from the organ grinder's pet. Outraged by the attack, the child's father rushed out and stabbed the monkey to death. The onlookers, instead of berating the organ grinder for letting his pet bite the child, at once set up a collection for the busker and his late, lamented monkey, and plans were put in motion to give the unfortunate animal a decent funeral. So much money was raised that booze and food were bought and a celebratory wake was held with singing, dancing and drinking. The funeral wake was so successful that the townsfolk decided to celebrate the monkey's stabbing every year on the anniversary of the incident. It is said that the first person to become totally drunk during the festivities can become Mayor of Chalvey for a year. Today the locals are still referred as the Stab Monks – or should that be the drunk mayors?

Following county boundary changes in 1974, Chalvey was removed, no doubt with a sigh of relief in Aylesbury, from Buckinghamshire and transferred to Berkshire.

1914–1918

THE GREAT WAR

ALONGSIDE A PATHWAY which leads from the car park to the summit of Whiteleaf Hill above Princes Risborough there lie, hidden amongst trees and undergrowth, a line of depressions, mounds and hollows which – to the untrained eye – would appear to be the natural rise and fall of the land. In fact, these contours are man-made, and they look out over a landscape of fields, backed by woods, which would in time become chillingly familiar to the men who dug them 100 years ago. For these are practice trenches excavated by locally garrisoned soldiers who, in August 1914, would soon be ordered to France to confront the German war machine, where many of them would die in the struggle.

Practice trenches dug in 1914 on top of Whiteleaf Hill by soldiers soon sent to fight in France.

Soldiers looking over the top of the trenches.

The outbreak of the First World War in 1914 did not initially impinge on Buckinghamshire. It was a distant conflict concerning old empires, ancient European families and the imperial designs of rising military powers, which had little or no interest to the people of Bucks. Yet by the war's end four years later, every hamlet, village and town in the county would have been affected by the tragedy.

The eagerness to serve king and country was soon lost amid the horrors of the battlefield, where nineteenth-century field tactics were hopelessly out of sync with murderous weapons of mass industrialisation. Thousands of young men were cut down by machine guns, mortar and artillery before they got more than 100 feet from their trenches.

Throughout Buckinghamshire the many war memorials tell a familiar, bloody story. In Stewkley, thirty men would never return; in Wendover, fifty-eight; in Bletchley, sixty-eight; in Swanbourne, sixty-five; in Newport Pagnell, 130; in Wolverton, 130; in West Wycombe, seventy-eight; in Waddesdon, sixy-five; in Chesham, 185 ... the list goes on.

The cost of the Great War was on an unprecedented and unimaginable scale. We can gain some idea of the extent of the carnage when we look at the British Army's most bloody day: the Battle of the Somme, which took place from July through to November 1916. On the first day some 60,000 soldiers were either killed or wounded. That is the equivalent of the combined populations of Marlow, Beaconsfield, Buckingham, Olney and Winslow being cut down in less than 14 hours. By the end of the battle five months later, the losses had risen to 420,000 British soldiers, a figure comparable to the combined number of residents of Milton Keynes, Aylesbury and High Wycombe. If one adds the German and French dead to the casualty list, the number of deaths is equivalent to the entire population of modern-day Buckinghamshire. And at the end of the battle, after the sacrifice of so many lives, only 7 miles of territory had been won.

It was men of the Oxfordshire and Buckinghamshire light infantry who entered this butcher's yard; they suffered many casualties, in particular at Delville Wood (renamed by troops, for good reason, as Devil's Wood). The Ox and Bucks were again to suffer extensive losses at the Battle of Beaumont Hamel on 13 November.

They had shown their metal during the early days of the conflict. In August 1914, the 2nd Ox and Bucks arrived on the Western Front, as part of the 5th Infantry Brigade, 2nd Division, 1st Corps. It was one of the first divisions of the British Expeditionary force (BEF) to arrive in France under the command of Sir John French, a resident of Fenny Stratford near Bletchley. The battalion took part in the first British battle of the war at Mons in Belgium, where the British defeated the German forces that they had encountered on 23 August. The battalion subsequently took part in halting the German advance at the crucial Battle of the Marne, from 5–9 September 1915.

Sir John French in Paris. (LOC, LC-DIG-ggbain-17041)

Cliveden House stands on the banks of the River Thames near Taplow in south Buckinghamshire. Designed in the English Palladian style by Sir Charles Barry in 1851, it is the third building to occupy the site. The first, built in 1666, and home to George Villiers, 2nd Duke of Buckingham, burned down in 1795 and the second house, constructed in 1824, was also destroyed by fire in 1849. Throughout its history the house has been associated with the titled, rich and famous.

In 1893 the estate was purchased by a very wealthy American, William Waldorf Astor, later to become 1st Lord Astor. He lived at Cliveden as a recluse after the death of his wife and gave the house to his son, Waldorf, as a wedding present following his marriage to American socialite Nancy Langhorne in 1906.

Although she was not the first woman to be elected to parliament, Nancy Langhorne Astor was the first female to sit in the House of Commons when she was chosen to represent Plymouth in November 1919. Today she is mostly remembered for her association with 'the Cliveden set', as much a disparate group of individuals as one could imagine; they included film stars, politicians, world leaders, writers and artists. The heyday of entertaining at Cliveden was between the two world wars when the Astors held regular weekend parties, which were attended by such people as Charlie Chaplin, Winston Churchill, Joseph Kennedy, the father of President Robert Kennedy, Ghandi, Lawrence of Arabia, Franklin D. Roosevelt, and Rudyard Kipling.

Nancy Langhorne Astor was suspected of having Nazi sympathies and of being Hitler's woman in Britain, and yet she commented that the leader of the third Reich looked too much like Charlie Chaplin to be taken seriously. On one occasion she had the nerve – or the foolishness – to ask Communist dictator Joseph Stalin, to his face, why he had murdered so many Russians …

Nancy Astor and her second husband and family in 1922. (LOC, LC-DIG-npcc-22736)

On 31 October the Germans launched a large-scale attack against General Sir Douglas Haig's 1st Corps in the area of Ypres, which commenced with a heavy bombardment followed by a mass infantry attack. Yet it was halted by two companies of the 2nd Ox and Buckinghamshire, and a subsequent counter-attack forced the enemy back to their front line. On 11 November the Germans made another attempt to capture Ypres, sending the elite Prussian Guard against the British forces. Once again the 2nd Battalion counter-attacked, preventing their advance and then routing them. The 2nd Ox and Bucks sustained 632 casualties during the first five months of the war. Over the following four years almost 6,000 Buckinghamshire men would perish in battle – a mercifully low number given the carnage which ensued.

The war didn't discriminate between rich and poor. In 1878, Hannah, the daughter of Baron Mayer de Rothschild, who had built Mentmore Towers in the 1850s, married Archchibald Primrose, 5th Earl of Rosebery. Four years later, in 1882, they were blessed with a son, Neil James Archibald Primrose. In November 1917, Captain James Primrose led the Royal Buckinghamshire Hussars at the battle of El Mughar in Palestine. At first trotting, then galloping, they gained the crest of the ridge, but at the cost of 16 killed, 114 wounded and 265 horses. It was the last cavalry charge ever made by the British Army. Primrose was among the dead, and lies buried near Ramla. His family erected a plaque to his memory in Mentmore church.

When the guns fell silent on the eleventh hour of the eleventh day of the eleventh month in 1918, the world, Britain and Buckinghamshire had become a different place. Many of the soldiers who had dug the practice trenches up on Whiteleaf Hill did not return home. Gone were the men, and the innocence. It was the war to end all wars. Surely most people must have thought such savagery could not be repeated, but within twenty years they would be proved wrong – and this time, for the people of Buckinghamshire, the war was much closer to home.

AD 1923–1962

DUNSMORE'S
DOOMED DAREDEVIL

SOMETIMES PEOPLE'S EXPLOITS would seem to be more at home in the work of a Hollywood screenwriter. The extraordinary nature of their tale makes one wonder if the whole yarn was invented. One such story concerns the incredible adventures of intrepid Buckinghamshire flyer Captain Bill Lancaster, one-time resident of Dunsmore and Monks Risborough. His amazing career combined the daring-do of Biggles, the adventurousness of Lawrence of Arabia and the stupidity of Laurel and Hardy.

Bill Lancaster was born in Birmingham in 1898, the son of an electrical engineer. In his teens he emigrated to Australia where he worked for a time on a sheep station. Aged 18 he joined the Australian Calvary and became an accomplished horseman. At the outset of the First World War he sought a chance to return to Britain and transferred to the Australian Air Force, where he soon became a fully trained pilot and was commissioned as a second lieutenant. In 1918 he received a commission in the Royal Air Force and was posted to India. He returned to

England in 1923 and was posted to RAF Halton, near Wendover. At the tender age of 25, Lancaster had already led a colourful existence and yet life was to become even more exhilarating for the go-get-it captain – with success, triumph, heartbreak and, ultimately, disaster.

Bill Lancaster was happy at Halton. His social circle widened and he enjoyed the company of his fellow offices. However, not all extended the warm hand of friendship to him: he was seen by the other men as something of a bighead, always showing off. In 1924 he boasted that he could beat the other contestants at a London Rodeo by staying on the bucking broncos the longest. The men at Halton encouraged him to take part, hoping that he would fail. But he didn't. He won the challenge dressed in a pinstripe suit and bowler hat.

Even though the dashing captain's daring exploits gave him a sense of adventure, what he really wanted was to make his name as an aeronaut, and be the first man to fly from England to Australia. But finance was a problem. In 1927 he met a vivacious 25-year-old Australian divorcee, Jessie 'Chubbie' Miller, who managed to obtain the money for Lancaster's project and said she would like to accompany him. On the afternoon of 14 October 1927, they set off in an Avro Avian aircraft for the 20,000-mile flight to Darwin. Things soon began to go wrong. On the first leg of the journey they had to make an emergency landing short of the airfield in France. Here the take-off space was too limited for the plane with a full load – so Lancaster forced Chubbie out and told her to walk to the airfield!

They continued the journey over the desert, but ran into sandstorms and were shot at by tribesmen. When they reached Basra they were strongly advised not to cross the Persian Gulf, but the daring captain took no notice and set off across shark-infested waters. Halfway out the engine began to cough and splutter, and it was only Lancaster's skill in controlling the stalling aircraft that saved them from becoming a Great White's smörgåsbord. When they reached Calcutta on 19 December, Lancaster persuaded Chubbie to take the controls. They took off and the control stick jammed, immediately plunging the plane into a nosedive. By a miracle, they managed to avoid certain death.

As they flew over Rangoon the engine packed up again, yet once again they managed to land unscathed. Undaunted by such bad luck, they took off on the last 3,000 miles of the flight. However, once airborne Chubbie got the shock of her life when she found her rear cockpit had become infested with snakes. With great bravery and a little panic, she managed to kill them with a stick. They landed at Singapore, but eager to make up time they at once took to the skies. Yet they

had only gone 150 feet when the engine failed and they came crashing down to earth. Chubbie escaped unhurt, but Lancaster was injured.

Incredibly, after recuperating they continued on their perilous journey. Over Sumatra, the plane's engine again gave trouble but they made it to Darwin in late March 1928. However, there was no one there to welcome them; the crowd, fed up with waiting for the two aeronauts, had gone home. Nonetheless, Lancaster and Chubbie were heroes. Their epic hazardous journey had also brought them together and they fell in love.

They eventually went to America where they met a young, good-looking writer called Haden Clarke who moved in with the two flyers. Unhappily for Lancaster, Chubbie fell for the charming Clarke and they became lovers. The Dunsmore captain was devastated. He pleaded for Chubbie to return with him to England, but she was intent on marrying the handsome American.

It was not to be. On the night of 20 April 1932, Clarke was found dead in bed from a shotgun wound to his head. The gun belonged to Lancaster, and beside the body were two suicide notes: one addressed to Chubbie, the other to Lancaster. The notes were found to be forgeries written by the captain and he was arrested and put on trial. Despite the damaging evidence against him, Lancaster's defence proved that Clarke had killed himself, and the captain was acquitted.

Lancaster returned to Britain without Chubbie, where the spectre of Clarke's death hung over him, and he was shunned. He was, however,

There are many test and fighter pilots the world over who owe a debt of gratitude to a man who lies buried in a peaceful Buckinghamshire churchyard – perhaps none more so than an American astronaut. Just a few months before Neil Armstrong set foot on the surface of the moon, he was test flying a version of the lunar module when it went out of control and plummeted to the ground. But for his ejector seat, Armstrong would have been killed. The man who invented the seat was engineer and inventor Sir James Martin, whose grave is in Old Denham churchyard. Martin's company still operates at Higher Denham.

still desperate to undertake another ambitious flight to regain his honour. With money from his father, Lancaster planned to break Amy Johnson's speed record for a flight from England to South Africa. On 11 April 1933, with some chicken sandwiches and chocolate from his mother, he set off from Hampshire on the epic flight to Cape Town. Yet, as before, he ran into trouble. Over North Africa sandstorms blew him off course and after 20 hours he was forced down at Reggane in Algeria. The sandstorms became worse, and Lancaster was told it was madness to attempt to fly in such conditions. But the captain was desperate to make up time. The officials informed him that he would surely become lost at night over the Sahara desert; he didn't even have an illuminated instrument panel. Lancaster replied that he could easily read the panel with his matches. Shaking their heads in disbelief, the officials watched as the captain took off into the ferocious stormy night. He was never seen alive again.

In February 1962, a French army patrol came across a crashed plane in a vast and trackless part of the Sahara Desert known as the 'Land of Thirst' by the local Bedouin. Besides the wreckage was the mummified body of Bill Lancaster. He had survived the crash, but waited in vain in the scorching desert for help. He lasted eight days. His last diary entry read, 'Keeping my chin up.'

AD 1941

THE BABES IN THE WOOD

ON 19 NOVEMBER 1941, 6-year-old Kathleen Trendle and Doreen Hearne, aged 8, were on their way home from Tyler's Green School in Penn, near High Wycombe. They had reached the crossroads by Elm Road and Common Wood Lane when an army truck pulled up beside them. The driver leaned out of his cab and offered the two girls a ride. Both got in, and the truck drove off in the direction of the Penn Street Village. The children did not return home that night; three days later their bodies were discovered in a nearby wood. Both had been strangled and stabbed.

Close by were the tyre tracks of a lorry and a large patch of oil. There was also Doreen's gas-mask holder and a khaki handkerchief with the laundry mark 'RA1019'. A 12-year-old boy told police that he saw the two girls getting into the truck, and gave the unit identification marks of the lorry. The vehicle was quickly traced to 341 Battery, 86 Field Regiment, Royal Artillery, in Yoxford, Suffolk, and police soon found the vehicle with a leaking back axle. The tyre tracks matched the impressions taken from the scene. The driver was 26-year-old gunner

Harold Hill. He had the laundry mark RA1019, and his fingerprints were found to match those on the discarded gas mask container. When his kit was examined, his spare uniform was found to have bloodstains on it. His plea of insanity was rejected and he was hanged at Oxford Castle on 1 May 1942.

A curious postscript to this dreadful murder occurred many years after the tragic event. On an October night in 1995, a metal detectorist went to Penn, eager to explore the adjacent fields for ancient artefacts lost over the years. After an hour of fruitless searching he decided to pack up and return home. He made his way back into the woods and down to his car. He had only gone a little way into the trees when he heard voices: the laughter and shouts of children. He was puzzled. What were children doing in a wood at that hour? The voices seemed to be coming closer, so he remained still and continued to listen. Then he heard them again – this time behind him. He quickly spun around. The laughter and singing of the children rapidly headed in his direction, but there was no accompanying sounds of snapping twigs or the rustle of bushes.

They met in 1934 and fell madly in love. She was Lady Georgiana Curzon, the eldest daughter of the 5th Earl Howe, who lived at Penn House in the village of Penn Street near Amersham. He was a dashing RAF pilot from South Africa by the name of Roger Bushell. Despite the couple's love for each other, Georgiana's father was unimpressed by Bushell's social standing and did not approve, forcing the couple to part.

Georgiana was heartbroken and eventually went on to marry the son of a motor-racing friend of Earl Howe, but it was a disaster. She obtained a divorce in 1941 after her new husband admitted committing adultery with her stepmother.

A year earlier Bushell's spitfire had been shot down in France. He escaped from three prisoner-of-war camps before being recaptured and, while in hiding, sent vital information back to Britain through coded letters, including notes on development of V-bomb rockets. Whilst in captivity, Bushell continually told other prisoners that 'Georgie' was his true love whom he would one day marry. Tragically, they were never to meet again: Bushell was one of the fifty escapees murdered by the Gestapo in 1944. The story was told in the film *The Great Escape*, in which Richard Attenborough played the part of Bushell (who master-minded the breakout by co-ordinating the digging of three tunnels, Tom, Dick and Harry).

Georgiana found it hard to accept that Bushell would never return. Every year for years she placed an 'In Memoriam' in *The Times* on his birthday, ending with the words 'Love is Immortal' and signed 'Georgie'. Her gravestone in Holy Trinity, Penn Street, is marked with two lines of poetry by Tennyson: 'Oh for the touch of a vanished hand, and the sound of a voice that is still.'

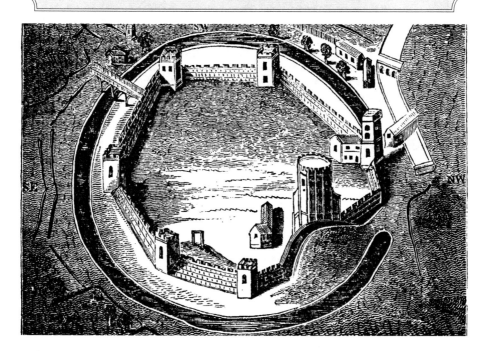

Early view of Oxford Castle, where Hill was hanged.

On the night of 7 August 1963 a mail train left Glasgow at 6.50 p.m. en route to Euston Station in London carrying £2.6 million (worth £46 million today) in bank notes that were to be destroyed. It was due to arrive in London at 3.59 a.m., and its journey south went without incident until, 40 minutes before arriving at its destination, a signal at red halted the train at Sears Crossing near the village of Cheddington. Several masked men entered the cab and coshed the driver over the head, rendering him unconscious. The driver's mate, who had climbed down from the cab to call the signalman from a railway trackside telephone (only to find the cables had been cut), was grabbed from behind as he made his way back to the train and quickly overpowered by one of the men.

The engine and the first two coaches of the train were uncoupled and driven half a mile further up the track to Bridego bridge, where fifteen robbers smashed their way into the carriages containing the money and proceeded to unload 120 sackfuls of loot into three waiting vehicles. The robbery had taken just under 30 minutes, and soon the men – and the millions – had sped off through the Buckinghamshire night to their planned hideout 27 miles from the crime scene at Leatherslade Farm, between Brill and Long Crendon.

Knowing that the police would expect them to return to London with the money, the robbers made their way to the farm by empty country roads, passing through the villages of Wingrave, Aston Abbots, Cublington, Oving, Upper Winchendon and Chilton.

At Leatherslade Farm the money was shared out, with each robber getting £90,000. After lying low for a few days, the gang members took their share of the spoils and made their own getaways. The police, however, were soon on to them. The Leatherslade hideout was quickly located, and damning fingerprint evidence at the scene was obtained which would lead to the conviction of the criminals.

The leader of the gang, Bruce Reynolds (his son, Nick Reynolds, is a member of the pop group Alabama 3 who wrote the theme music to the hit American show *The Sopranos*) escaped abroad, as did Buster Edwards, the robber who was said to have coshed the train driver. The most famous of the robbers, Ronnie Biggs, managed to escape justice for over forty years before he gave himself up, an old and broken man. The rest of the gang were eventually captured, and at Aylesbury Crown Court on 15 April 1964, after a trial lasting fifty-one days, were sentenced to terms ranging from three to thirty years' imprisonment. However, it is believed that three unidentified robbers managed to evade the police, and remain free to this day.

The Great Train Robbery, more than any other modern crime, caught the public's imagination for its daring and scale, and has inspired many books, plays and films.

Today, even though Leatherslade Farm has been demolished, Bridego Bridge, renamed Train Robbers' Bridge, remains and it's still possible for crime buffs to visit the scene of the greatest robbery Buckinghamshire has ever known.

Thirty years ago the author of this book became friends with one of the Great Train Robbers. In 1982, whilst living in Camberwell, south London, Buster Edwards was my next-door neighbour. He was a pleasant chap, and though we chatted many times about numerous subjects he never once talked about that fateful night in 1963. Sadly, Edwards committed suicide in 1994.

Buster Edwards.
(With kind permission
of Andrew Cook, from
his volume The Great
Train Robbery*)*

⸺⸺

Travellers passing through Burnham Beeches near Slough could well be forgiven for thinking they were in the depths of Transylvania, and that Count Dracula or Frankenstein's monster could at any moment leap from the shadows. In fact they wouldn't be far wrong, as the woods have been used on many occasions as locations for the popular Hammer horror films of the '60s and '70s, as well as the Harry Potter series. Indeed South Buckinghamshire could well be considered Britain's Hollywood as, down the years, numerous blockbuster movies have been produced at Pinewood, Beaconsfield and Denham studios. Latterly, locations such as Little Missenden, Bledlow, Chesham, Turville and Quainton have all featured in the ever-popular *Midsomer Murders*, and *The Vicar of Dibley*.

⸺⸺

Just as quickly as the voices had sounded behind him, they immediately changed course, floating from the direction of the fields, seemingly fading and then coming near. Then the sound of the children seemed to be all around him and the detectorist became scared. He fled down through the wood and back to his car, got in and, before starting the engine, wound the window down. He listened. There were no sounds coming from the wood: only the wind in the trees. He quickly drove away, his eyes on the road, expecting at any moment to see two ghostly children walk out in front of him. Is it possible that he had heard the spirits of the two children murdered in 1941?

AD 1939–1945

BUCKINGHAMSHIRE DOES ITS BIT

T HE SECOND WORLD WAR, it can be argued, was in reality the continuation of the first, but with a twenty-one-year interval. The terms, conditions and reparation payments demanded by the victorious Allies, together with the stock market crash of the 1930s, forced a defeated Germany into economic catastrophe from which Adolph Hitler elbowed his way to power. He then dragged the world into six years of bloody misery.

Unlike the 1914–18 conflict, the people of Buckinghamshire would come to experience the Second World War up close and personal. Neville Chamberlain's 1939 declaration that Britain was at war with Germany was followed by a Blitzkrieg, which saw most of Europe fall under the darkness of the swastika. By early 1940, Hitler's forces were poised to cross the English Channel. Two thousand years earlier Julius Caesar had stood on the same shore with the same intention. Back then, the Roman general was confronted by Celtic tribes under the leadership of the Catuvellauni. In 1940 the Nazi leader would face a nation which had forged itself into a formidable fighting race determined to defend their island at all costs.

But he had to gain control of the air before an invasion could be launched. The Luftwaffe were defeated in the Battle of Britain, probably the most pivotal battle of the Second World War. If Britain had fallen there would have been no springboard from which the Allies could launch the Normandy landings and free Europe.

Thwarted in their attempts to knock out the RAF, the Germans resorted to bombing Britain's towns and cities. London suffered the most and Londoners fleeing the Blitz came to Buckinghamshire. Hospitals, schools and factories were also relocated to escape the nightly onslaught.

They had come to avoid the bombs, yet the enemy planes delivered their deadly cargo all over the county. Although the German High Command considered many of these raids as mistaken targets, their explosive power was not lost on the people. Over 1,700 bombs and almost 4,000 incendiaries were dropped on Buckinghamshire between 1940 and 1943. Thirty-three people were killed and 200 houses destroyed.

In 1942, A V2 rocket (flying bomb) aimed at London overshot its target and landed on Castlefield School in High Wycombe. Mercifully, no one was killed.

Ironically the greatest loss of life in Buckinghamshire from a wartime incident did not come from enemy bombing, but from an Allied plane crash. On the night of Saturday, 7 August 1943, a Wellington bomber which had taken off from Wing airfield at 1.25 a.m. on a night training flight got into trouble over Winslow. As it came down it hit the roofs of several buildings in the high street before crashing into a pub. Seventeen people died, including the plane's crew and a family of Jewish evacuees who had moved from London to Winslow to escape the Blitz.

If Britain couldn't hit back at the enemy through military means, there was always covert action. The country houses of Buckinghamshire played a vital part in the intelligence war against Nazi Germany. Hughenden Manor, once the home of Victorian Prime Minister Benjamin Disraeli, became 'station hillside'. It was here that reconnaissance photographs of the Ruhr dams were analysed, which helped formulate the plans for the famous Dam Buster raid on the Ruhr Valley in Germany in 1943.

Wingrave Manor in the village of Aston Abbots became, in 1940, the headquarters of the exiled Czech government under the leadership of President Eduard Benes. It was at Wingrave that the assassination of

Plane wreckage and destroyed houses in Winslow.

Hughenden Manor. (Courtesy of Simon Quinton)

Bletchley Park where the Enigma code was deciphered.

Aerial view of the D-Day landings. (LOC, LC-USZ62-111201)

Reinhold Heydrich, the Nazi butcher of Bohemia and possible successor to Hitler, was planned. Heydrich was killed, but the people of Czechoslovakia paid a terrible price for his death.

Perhaps the most famous of all Buckinghamshire country house locations to play its part in the covert war was Bletchley Park. Codenamed Ultra, the Victorian mansion was the home of the code breakers headed by mathematics genius Alan Turing, considered by many to be the father of the modern computer. It was at Bletchley that the German Enigma code was broken and deciphered, allowing the British to read every message and order sent out to German commanders in the field. The intelligence work at Bletchley Park is thought to have shortened the war by two years.

Although covert actions would thwart and delay the enemy, the real victory would only come with the combined force of army, navy and air force. The men of Buckinghamshire had already shown their metal during the withdrawal to Dunkirk. In May 1940 the 1st Buckinghamshire Battalion were given the job of defending the Belgium town of Hazebrouck, where they were confronted by German panzers and thousands of troops. The 1st Buckinghamshire were armed with only rifles and grenades, yet they managed to halt the advancing Nazis for a crucial 48 hours, allowing the British Expeditionary Force time to evacuate more men.

Pegasus Bridge.

Another wartime operation all Buckinghamshire people can be proud of was carried out by the men of the Ox and Bucks Light Infantry on the night of 5 June 1944. A force of 181 men, led by Major John Howard, took off from southern England in six gliders to capture Pegasus Bridge over the Orne River. The force was composed of D Company, 2nd Battalion. Their D-Day mission was to take and secure the bridge and prevent German armour from crossing the river and attacking the eastern flank of the Allied landings on Sword beach.

Just after midnight on 6 June, five of the Ox and Bucks' gliders landed as close as 47 yards from their objectives,

taking the German defenders completely by surprise. Within 10 minutes they had taken and secured the bridge. In the short but fierce battle they lost Lieutenant Den Brotheridge, a one-time council employee at Aylesbury, who was killed in the first minutes of the assault. The heroic lieutenant became the first member of the invading Allied armies to be killed in action on D-Day and was posthumously awarded the Military Cross.

Sir Winston Churchill had warned the Nazis that the British people would fight in the fields and in the streets and in the hills, and that we would never surrender. He was proved quite right, because the people of Buckinghamshire did their bit.

Also from The History Press

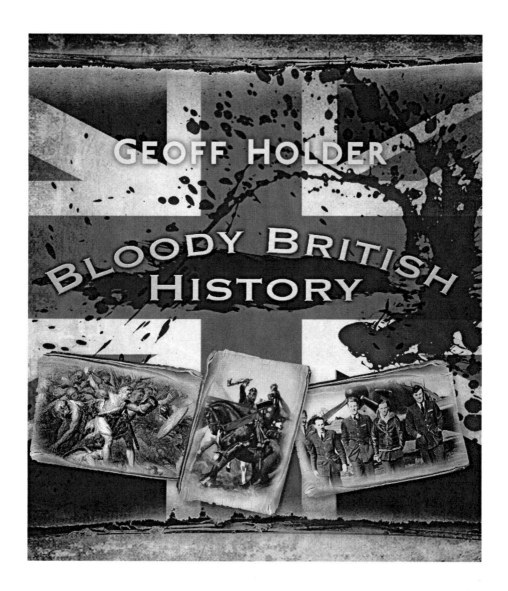

GEOFF HOLDER

BLOODY BRITISH HISTORY

Find this title and more at

www.thehistorypress.co.uk

Lightning Source UK Ltd.
Milton Keynes UK
UKOW05f1530151014

240130UK00001B/1/P